2/00

come alive!

frances hunter

Published by Bible Voice Books
P.O. Box 7491
Van Nuys, Calif. 91409

INDEX

INTRODUCTION

Jesus Christ is the most EXCITING person I've ever met! If you want adventure, Christian life is the most adventuresome life in the world! If you're bored—it will take the boredom out of life. If you want love—there is no love like the love of God as He wraps His arms around you. When the problems of life come up, just ask the Lord to put His arms of love around you a little tighter, and squeeze you a little harder, and somehow in His great and mighty love, all problems will be solved.

If you want a life that is daring—I challenge anyone to the Christian life. There are moments when great daring is needed—and yet these are the moments when Jesus is felt the most in our lives because He never fails us.

If you want the unusual—Christianity can give you the most unusual life in the world—in a "fabulous" way.

If you want a challenging life—Jesus will give you just that.

If you would dare to be different—the Christian life is different!

So put them all together, and if in one single life you want excitement, adventure, love, daring, the unusual, freedom from boredom, challenge, and a life that's different —then just give Jesus the reins and see what happens.

Come Alive!

Of course, if you want a humdrum existence, a boring life with no adventure, no challenge, no excitement, then you'd better stop reading right now because you can have that kind of life all by yourself, without any outside help!

LET JESUS COME ALIVE

It's been almost nine years since I came into a personal relationship with Jesus Christ, and the question that's asked me more than any other one is, "How do you stay on top all the time?" "Are you always like this?" Yes, beloved, I'm always like this. There isn't any reason for a Christian to ever be "down in the dumps." Now don't misunderstand me, I'm not saying you're not going to have any problems, because I've had more than my share since I became a Christian, but I'VE GOT THE ANSWER. Who cares how many problems you have when you've got the answer?

What would happen if I announced right now that all of you who wanted to have something to do tomorrow, could have a half-hour appointment with Jesus Christ? Suppose I told you He would be within walking distance of your house tomorrow and I'd be very glad to make an appointment for you to have a 30-minute counseling session with Him concerning your needs? You could counsel with Him about whatever subject you wanted to, you could counsel with Him about your needs, you could counsel with Him concerning your problems. Jesus is going to be available to you for personal counseling! How many of you would rush to get your name on that list so that you could be right here for the first appointment? Wouldn't we all really like to be where we could talk to Jesus in person?

May I suggest something? Start thinking about reading your Bible as being a personal counseling session with Jesus Christ! For every need that you have in your life, there is an answer wrapped up in the pages of this Book. There are so many people who don't believe it. Do you know why? They don't READ God's Word, and consequently when they don't read God's Word, they don't know what God has to say to them, but EVERY problem in today's living has an answer in this Book if we would just open it and read it. God tells each one of us how to have an exciting Christian life, if we will just open the Book and hear what He's got to say!

Another question that's asked almost as much as the first one as we travel around the country is, "How do I know what God wants out of my life? How do I know when God is speaking to me? How do I know what God is telling me to do?" The minute anyone says that to me, it tells me a real interesting thing. It says that person isn't reading God's Word enough!

From the moment I became a Christian, God instilled in my heart the most fanatical desire to read His Word. I couldn't stand it. . . . I thought the Bible was going to go out of print the next day! I thought they'd come and take all my Bibles away from me! I thought I'd never be able to read God's Word and I would never know what God wanted out of my life, so I literally chewed up God's Word. I just ate it up! Everywhere I went I had a Bible with me so that I could open it and see what God was saying to me.

God speaks to us in many different ways! People have sometimes said to me, "Does God come out of the woodwork and say, 'Frances, I want you to do this'?" No, God has never come out of the woodwork and has never spoken to me like that. I'm sure that there are those whom God has spoken to in an audible voice. God has spoken to

Charles and called him by name, but God has never spoken to me that way.

Many times God speaks to us in the form of an instantaneous thought. We pray. God answers us, and then the very next thing that happens is the old devil comes and throws in that second thought! Then we get all confused and think, "Now which one was God?" "Which one of those two was really God?" Let me just tell you this. If you're really in earnest with God, the first voice will always be from God. The first one will always be positive. But watch out for that second one, because when the second one comes in there, you begin to get so confused you say, "Who was first?" Then you lose track. Listen carefully for that small, still voice of God.

God also uses people many times in our lives to let His message come through to our hearts, and He really uses His Word.

The most neglected area in the lives of the "defeated" Christians is probably Bible reading. It shouldn't be! This should be the most exciting, stimulating part of your day, or at least one of the most exciting parts. And it can be if you'll do just a few things. I guarantee you if you'll do what I tell you, Jesus and James and John and Peter will all come alive and romp across the pages of your Bible, just like they walk through the pages of mine. Now don't tell me you don't have time, because nobody "has" time.

Did you know that "almost 30 percent of all 66 books in the Old and New Testaments have fewer than six chapters that are easily read in less than 20 minutes? During the time required to read ten pages in tonight's newspaper, you can read the almost 40,000 words which make up all 150 Psalms? Staggering, isn't it? . . . Ten of the shortest books come from the Old Testament and 14 are found in the New Testament.

"Any of these books can be read in less time than it takes to watch 30 minutes of any television program. The volumes include Ruth, Lamentations, Joel, Obadiah, Jonah, Nahum, Habakkuk, Zephaniah, Haggai, Malachi, Philippians, Colossians, I & II Thessalonians, II Timothy, Titus, Philemon, James, I & II Peter, the three epistles of John, and Jude.

"Issues explored in these 300 to 3,000 word capsules from God include care of in-laws (Ruth), misplaced priorities in missionary strategy (Jonah), corruption on Capitol Hill (Nahum), money management (Malachi), sex roles in marriage (Colossians), how to suffer successfully (I Peter), and others.

"Dr. G. Campbell Morgan, noted English author, once reported that a person can read every verse from Genesis through Revelation in approximately 80 hours. . . . One study conducted by the U.S. Army Signal Corps indicates that the average American reads only one book and 57 magazine articles per year, but watches more than 12,000 (sic) hours of television."*

So the answer to Bible reading lies in how much you really *want* to read your Bible. How much of your time do you spend watching TV? How much of the newspaper do you really need to read? The last time I read the newspaper, someone was murdered, someone was raped, someone committed a burglary and had been caught, and someone had died from an overdose of drugs. I decided to spend my time reading God's Word where I could find things that would build me up instead of letting me down!

It all started when I was a new Christian and I had this tremendous hungering in my heart for God's Word, and then someone told me that there were over 70,000 promises in God's Holy Word, and I remember thinking, "Seventy thousand all for me?" Then I said, "Lord, let me live long enough to claim all those promises." I don't really know if there actually are that many (or more) in the Bible, but all I

Christian Life, January 1975, "Bible Reading; Short and Sweet" by John N. Vaughan.

can say is "Praise the Lord" that someone gave me that figure because it really started me in the Bible. After all, if God had 70,000 promises for me, how could I possibly know what they were unless I read His Word to find out what promises I could claim? So I started! I guess maybe because I was selfish it started me to be a fanatic about reading God's Holy Word.

When you read the Bible, read it seeking GOD! This is where so many people get hung up. They get all involved in seeking and learning knowledge. I've heard some great theologians talk who knew about all the verses in the Bible; they knew when Paul went where, and they knew where and when Peter went, but they didn't know Jesus! They didn't know Jesus! Why? Because they read the Bible seeking knowledge instead of seeking God. IF YOU WANT TO END UP A THEOLOGIAN, THAT'S GREAT. Study it that way, but I'll let you in on a little secret. If I were somebody who didn't have a lot of time, I'd study it one way, just seeking God, because you have no idea what can happen to you when you do.

There are only four little points I'm going to give you, but they can revolutionize your entire life, if you will read this carefully. Many people "know" the Bible and can quote verses, but they don't know how to apply it to daily living. They don't know a LIVING Jesus, and there's all the difference in the world in just reading Scriptures or letting them come alive in your own life.

First of all, it's important to spend at least an hour a day in the Bible. And I don't mean breaking it up into 15-minute segments. It really takes you 15 minutes to get into the Word of God and to get all the things of the day out of your mind. Did you know that? There is that point when you can be so completely submerged in God's Word and in His will and in worshiping Him that everything else is taken away and you're really in the spirit, but you don't get there the minute you open your Bible. That's why you should set aside one hour of uninterrupted reading.

Now I know this is hard if you have little children, but you can always get up an hour earlier in the morning; you can always stay up an hour later at night. Charles likes to get up at 5:30 in the morning. That's when he does his special Bible reading alone. We read the Bible together a lot, but we usually do that at night. I do most of my Bible reading during the day because I have a little more time in the daytime than Charles. When I used to work in my printing office before Charles and I were married, I read my Bible at night because that was when I got the most out of it. During those hours when everyone else was sound asleep, I could just crawl into God's Word. Then it was "You and me, Lord" and that's all. Find somewhere in your day an hour that you can set aside to get into God's Word if you want the real abundant life.

Second, I praise the Lord for the pastor of the little church where I became a Christian. I praise God because He sent me some people who really had a tremendous effect on my life, especially when I was a new Christian. I had a *King James Bible* that had been given to me in 1924, and I really treasured this beautiful Bible. I took extremely good care of it! As a matter of fact, I didn't want to wear it out, so I never read it. *I really wanted to take good care of it!* Even the gold was never cracked on my Bible.

I'll have to be real honest and tell you this, I never could understand the *King James* version. *The Revised Standard Version* had become very popular by the time I became a Christian, so I asked my pastor if he would select a version for me that he thought I would really understand because in my heart was created this desire for God's Word, and yet for some reason or other, *King James* just didn't go over with me. I tried to read it, but I didn't get very far. He went to the Bible bookstore and picked out a *Revised Standard* for me and I'll never forget the day he gave it to me. He brought it into the office and handed it to me, but he didn't really give it to me. He held tightly to the one side and said, "Frances, don't you DARE (and he scared me to death the way he said it) ever open this book without asking God's Holy Spirit to reveal the truth to you."

The Bible is nothing but a bunch of printed words upon plain old paper until God's Holy Spirit reveals the truth to you. Who is the Spirit of Truth? The Holy Spirit. "When the Holy Spirit, who is truth, comes, he shall guide you into all truth, for he will not be presenting his own ideas, but will be passing on to you what he has heard." (John 16:13) The Holy Spirit is the ONLY person who can reveal the truth of the Bible to you. The Bible ought to be as easy to understand as a first-grade reader, and it is, *if* you will ask the Holy Spirit to reveal the truth to you. I hope you'll remember to never open the Bible without asking the Spirit of God to reveal the truth to you. I guess my pastor really did a good job in impressing me with this fact, because I never open the Bible without asking the Holy Spirit's guidance. As a result, from that day on, the Bible became as easy to understand as a beautiful first-grade reader. That's probably the reason I LOVE to read the Bible, because it's so easy to understand.

Before you ever open your Bible, ask God to do something for you! Just pray a simple little prayer. "God, may Your Holy Spirit reveal the truth to me. What have You got for me today? Not yesterday, not last year, but TODAY?"

So many times people study the Bible and think it's so important to know where Paul went, and when. Did he go to Ephesus first, did he go to Galatia first, did he go to Thessalonica first . . . but may I ask you a question? Is that really important to you? Is it, when you're seeking God? Is that really important? Or is the important thing, "How did God use Paul to affect my life?" "How did God use Paul to say something that speaks to me today?" "How could He have said something 2,000 years ago that is relevant to me now, and answers whatever problem I've got in life today?" Read the Bible that way and see the answers you find!

There isn't anything in the Bible which would indicate that I'm scripturally correct on this third point, but I'm sure that God approves wholeheartedly. Whenever I'm reading the Bible, after I've asked God to reveal the truth to me, I get my little hot-pink pen out because I always underline. When I come across something that's good, I underline it once. When I come across something that's REAL good, I underline it two times. When I come across something that's out of sight, I underline it three times, and you should see a few places in my Bible where I have just underlined all over the place! Scribble, scribble, scribble! This means God really spoke to me through those verses.

How many of you have ever had a spiritual "down"? Did you ever have a day when you felt "blah"? The best way to get over feeling "blah" is to get into God's Holy Word, but don't go to a portion that you haven't underlined, or marked up in some special way. I'm always sure to stay out of the "begat" chapters, because there's nothing there that will turn you on and bring you out of the doldrums. Get into a portion that's all underlined, or all marked up. This means that God really spoke to you through a certain passage. When I need a spiritual lift, I go over to a part where God really spoke to me in an exciting way. I quickly thumb through and find a chapter that's all marked up because I know that God's got something special for me again.

Consider getting a new Bible every year. Do you know that we have a tendency to get hung up if we don't? We don't realize how many beautiful verses there are in the Bible. Did you notice we keep quoting the same verses year after year after year after year. I made up my mind that for the next year I'm going to use all new verses of Scripture! Don't throw out the old verses, but learn some new ones! The Bible is just loaded with some fantastic truths. The reason we suggest a new Bible is so that you can start underlining afresh and anew. You have no idea how your underlining will change from year to year. I look back at the *Revised Standard* that I carried when I first became a Christian. I still love the verses that I underlined then. But the verses that I left out are the ones that today I have underlined as being very important and very special. What's really amazing are the ones I left out!

You may never really grow the way you should if you just keep the same edition all the time. You'll always have a favorite, but I think it's fun to make a collection of Bibles. Every Christian ought to have every translation there is. There ought to be a Bible every place in your house where there's room! There ought to be a Bible by every telephone in the house, because somebody might call you who needs a verse of Scripture, and you don't want to have to say, "Wait until I go and find my Bible someplace." If you just put a Bible by every telephone in the house, I guarantee you that exciting things will happen to you! Your living room should have one, your bedrooms should most certainly have one, but do you know one of the best places to put a Bible? In your bathroom!

I was at a youth convention in Oklahoma once and I gave this talk on Bible reading. I often say if I only had one talk to give to a group I would share with them how to make Jesus come alive through the Word, so I told them to put a Bible in their bathroom because that's the best place I know of. There was a preacher sitting there who looked at me and thought, "Oooooooohhhhhhhh!" Later he said he thought I was sacrilegious when I suggested that, but after he'd been there all week long, he said, "Somehow or other you just bubbled over every morning and the love of God was so obvious in your life, I thought there must be something to it." He said, "I went home and sneaked a little tiny pocket testament and put it in a drawer in the bathroom." (He didn't want anyone to see it.) Six months later I saw him and he said, "You know, you were right. I've never read the Bible so much in my whole life as I have the last six months since I put one in the bathroom." Hallelujah! Try putting one in your bathroom.

Charles and I have stayed in the homes of many pastors across the nation and we have a little saying, "By their bathroom literature shall ye know them!" You have no idea what we have found in the bathrooms of pastors and the homes of well-known Christians! It seems to be an American pastime to read there, so why not put some good literature there to read!

The *fourth* thing I want you to remember is probably the most important of all, because this is where the secret of coming alive really comes in. I guess it was right after I became a Christian, I sneaked into the office early one morning. I had a big counter around my desk in the printing company and I always kept a Bible sticking under there, so when there weren't any customers around, I would quickly pull the Bible out and read one or two little verses. This particular morning God seemed to direct me to read in Galatians. I started reading the first chapter.

Many of the letters in the New Testament start with all the fancy greetings, "Hello my dear brothers and sisters, and uncles and aunts, and nieces and nephews, and Phoebe and Eunice and all the girls that work in Caesar's palace, in the garbage department, and washing dishes and so forth". . . . Then Paul would take up a few verses sending greetings from "all the dear brothers and sisters, and uncles and aunts, and nieces and nephews, and Phoebe and Eunice, and all the girls that work here and there." And I used to think, "Who needs to read that kind of stuff?" Those flowery greetings didn't turn me on at all. I guess I heard a sermon early in my Christian life on the subject of getting off the milk and getting onto the meat of God's Word. I always thought the flowery greetings were the "milky way" stuff and I was in a hurry to get down to the hamburger!

As I started reading Galatians this one day, I flew through all the flowery stuff and then got settled with my teeth into the meat. All of a sudden I heard the real small, still voice of God. Many times we don't hear that small voice

of God. It was so soft and quiet I could have passed it by
except that I was really listening, and God said, "Go back!" I
thought, "I wonder what I missed?" So I went back, and this
is the way I read it "Paulanapostle—notfrommennorthrough
man,butthroughJesusChristandGodtheFatherwhoraisedhim
fromthedead!" And that's just the way I read it, as fast as I
could, and all run together. Then I got down into the meat
again and once again I heard that small, still voice say, "Go
back!"

So I went back and thought, "Maybe I read it a little
too fast." So I read it a little slower, saying, "Paul, an
apostle—not from men nor through man, but through Jesus
Christ and God the Father, who raised him from the dead."
(RSV) And I said, "But God, I didn't know Paul. He died a
few years before I was born." I got down into the meat again
and again I heard God say, "Go back." I said, "God, that just
didn't do a thing for me," and then I heard something that
revolutionized my whole Bible reading. He said, "I'm talking
to YOU!" I had said "Paul's dead, I didn't know him." But
God said, "I'm talking to YOU!"

All of a sudden I realized that God didn't write the
Bible just for Paul and James and John and Peter. Paul didn't
write it just for Timothy. God wrote it through those men
for ME! My Bible is my personal love letter from God. Over
and over through the years since then I've heard God repeat
those words, "I'm talking to YOU!"

I really got excited! I looked around to make sure no
one was looking (I forgot that God was watching all the time)
and I did something I had never done in my life before. I
took a pencil (because I thought in case it's sacrilegious I can
erase it) and scratched out Brother Paul's name and put my
own name in the Bible. Very softly in pencil, I wrote
"Frances." Then I read that same verse of Scripture, and
listen to what it said now: "Frances, an apostle, not from
men nor through man (because who saved me? No man or
church ever saved me), but through Jesus Christ and God the

Father, who raised HER from the dead." You see, I had been spiritually dead all those years. Who commissioned me? Did a church? Did a pastor? No, God the Father and Jesus Christ were the ones who commissioned me.

I got so excited I started through my Bible and I scratched out everybody's name I could find and put my own in. Every time I came across James and John and Peter, etc., I just scratched them out and wrote Frances, Frances, Frances all through the Bible. Why? Because all of a sudden I realized that God was talking to me! Today when I read the Bible, God is talking to ME, and to no one else. He is not saying these words to His disciples. Jesus is saying these words to you and me today. That's why every problem that you have in life has an answer, and that answer is in God's Holy Word, and no place else. If people who have marriage problems (or any other problems) would only realize that God laid down the guidelines for marriage 2,000 years ago and has never changed them. No matter what today's circumstances are, God never changed His mind about the perfect plan for marriage. Those same rules, if we abide by them, will give each one of us a marriage that is as perfect as Adam and Eve's before they sinned.

I got so turned on, I didn't want to do anything but put my name in the Bible. However, let me tell you this. Don't put your name in the good places unless you're willing to put it in the "bad" ones! God can get very nasty in places. Try putting your name in First Corinthians. Get over there in Galatians where He's talking about those who are not filled with the Holy Spirit and God can really get nasty with you. But I praise Him for this, because He had to get nasty with me (and still does) before I accepted Jesus, and He had to make me see myself for just what I was, and not the way I thought I was. I had to see myself in real light, because His Holy Spirit revealed what I really was and not according to my own personal opinion. So I put my name in the "bad" places too. I just went through the Bible and really had fun.

I'd like to take a little verse of Scripture right now and show you the difference when you read something the way it was originally written in the Bible and the way it speaks to you when you make it personal. This is taken from *I Frances* 6:11-12. (That's what my Bible says.) Originally it said Timothy, but now it says *Frances.* When I first read it, this is what is said: "Oh, Timothy, you are God's man. Run from all these evil things and work instead at what is right and good, learning to trust him and love others, and to be patient and gentle. Fight on for God. Hold tightly to the eternal life which God has given you, and which you have confessed with such a ringing confession before many witnesses."

What good did it do me to have God tell Timothy that he was His man? What good did it do me to have God tell Timothy to run from all these evil things? It didn't do a bit of good, but listen when I put my own name in there. My Bible says: "Oh, *Frances,* you are God's woman." Now, He's talking to me. He says, "*Frances,* you run (not Timothy), YOU run from all these evil things and you work instead at what is right and good, learning to trust him and love others, and to be patient and gentle." He's not talking to Timothy to be patient and gentle and to love others. He's talking to Frances Hunter and He says, "*Frances,* YOU be patient, YOU be gentle, YOU love others." And then He says, "*Frances,* fight on for God." Not Timothy, because he died a long time ago; He's talking to ME! "*Frances,* YOU hold tightly to that eternal life which God has given you and which you have confessed with such a ringing confession before many witnesses." See how different the Bible becomes when you make it personal? As I said, God can step on your toes, but when you realize that all of His love is directed at you, then it becomes very vital.

Probably the greatest place in the Bible to start putting your own name is John 3:16. I remember learning this verse when I was a little kid going to Sunday School because my mother and daddy made me. I didn't enjoy it a bit and didn't get a thing out of it, but I could say things faster than anybody else, so I got a gold star for saying "ForGodsoloved theworldthathegavehisonlybegottensonthatwhosoeverbeliev-ethinhimshouldnotperishbuthaveeverlastinglife." That's exactly the way I said it and that's just exactly how much I got out of it. You know what John 3:16 says in my Bible? Remember, this is MY Bible. My personal love letter from God. My Bible says: "For God so loved FRANCES HUNTER that he gave his only begotten Son, that if Frances Hunter should believe in Him (and she does), she should not perish, but have everlasting life"! Hallelujah!

God said it to me in His Holy Word, and the day that you can understand that God's Word was written for you is the day His Word will turn your life upside down. Say that verse with me right now, will you? Close your eyes so you can close out the rest of the world and say it with your name in it. "For God so loved _____ that He gave His only begotten Son, that if _____ should believe in Him, he/she should not perish, but have everlasting life."

Doesn't that give you spiritual goose pimples? I have said that thousands of times and I have never said it but that I see Jesus on the cross, dying just for me. And you know what else I see? I see Jesus coming out of the tomb, just for me! Not for all the rest of you, but just for me. God would have done it if I'd been the only person in the whole world who'd ever been born! Just like God would have done it for you if you'd been the only person in the whole wide world! If there had never been another person born, God would have let Jesus die just for you!

I want to share one chapter in the Bible that I think is fantastically beautiful. God gave Charles and me a joint ministry when we were married, so there are many places in my Bible and in Charles' Bible where we have written "Charles and Frances" because we believe in the oneness of marriage! This is the seventeenth chapter of John, and I'm quoting from *The Living Bible:*

"When Jesus had finished saying all these things he looked up to heaven and said, 'Father, the time has come. Reveal the glory of your Son so that he can give the glory back to you. For you have given him authority over every man and woman in all the earth. He gives eternal life to each one you have given him. And this is the way to have eternal life—by knowing you, the only true God, and Jesus Christ, the one you sent to earth! I brought glory to you here on earth by doing everything you told me to. And now, Father, reveal my glory as I stand in your presence, the glory we shared before the world began.

" 'I have told *Charles and Frances* all about you. They were in the world, but then you gave them to me. Actually, *Charles and Frances* were always yours, and you gave them to me; and they have obeyed you. Now *Charles and Frances* know that everything I have is a gift from you, for I have passed on to *Charles and Frances* the commands you gave me; and they accepted them and know of a certainty that I came down to earth from you, and they believe you sent me.

" 'My plea is not for the world but for *Charles and Frances* whom you have given me because they belong to you. And *Charles and Frances,* since they are mine, belong to you; and you have given them back to me with everything else of yours (and really listen to this), and so *Charles and Frances* are my glory!' " (Charles and Frances are my glory! Bill is my glory, Ruth is my glory, Susan is my glory, Tom and Patty are my glory, Joan and Bob are my glory! That's what your Bible ought to say, whatever your name is!)

" 'Now I'm leaving the world, and leaving them behind, and coming to you. Holy Father, keep *Charles and Frances* in your own care—all those you have given me, so that they will be united just as we are, with none missing. During my time here I have kept safe within your family all of these you gave me. I guarded them so that not one perished, except the son of hell, as the Scriptures foretold.

" 'And now I am coming to you. I have told *Charles and Frances* many things while I WAS WITH THEM SO THAT THEY WOULD BE FILLED WITH MY JOY. I have given them your commands. And the world hates them because they don't fit in with it, just as I don't. I'm not asking you to take *Charles and Frances* out of the world, but to keep them safe from Satan's power. *Charles and Frances* are not part of this world any more than I am. (And to that I say Praise the Lord!) Make them pure and holy through teaching them your words of truth. As you sent me into the world, I am sending *Charles and Frances* into the world (and I want you to listen to this promise of the living Jesus Christ: He said), and I consecrate myself to meet *Charles and Frances'* need for growth in truth and holiness.' "

(Jesus said "I consecrate myself to meet *Charles and Frances'* need for growth in truth and holiness." *I* consecrate myself to meet *[whoever you are]* need for growth in truth and holiness. And let me tell you something I do not believe is preached enough in churches today is holy living. Oh, if we only understood the beauty of holiness. God says, "Be ye holy as I am holy," and Jesus Christ said, "I CONSECRATE myself to meet Charles and Frances' need for growth in truth and holiness.")

" 'I am not praying for *Charles and Frances* alone but also for the future believers who will come to me because of the testimony of these. My prayer for all of them is that they will be of one heart and mind, just as you and I are, Father—that just as you are in me and I am in you, so *Charles and Frances* will be in us, and the world will believe you sent me.

" 'I have given *Charles and Frances* the glory you gave me—the glorious unity of being one, as we are—I in *Charles and Frances* and you in me, all being perfected into one—so that the world will know you sent me and will understand that you love *Charles and Frances* as much as you love me. (Isn't that beautiful? As much as Jesus. He loves US as much as He loves Jesus.) Father, I want *Charles and Frances* with ME. (That turns me on! Jesus saying I want Charles and Frances with Him. The resurrected Son of the living God says He wants us up there with Him. Hallelujah!)—these you've given me—so that they can see my glory. You gave me the glory because you loved me before the world began!

" 'O righteous Father, the world doesn't know you, but I do; and *Charles and Frances* know you sent me. And I have revealed you to them, and will keep on revealing you so that the mighty love you have for me may be in *Charles and Frances,* and I in them.' "

That's one chapter in the Bible made personal. Will you make your own Bible personal? Your Bible is God speaking directly to you. The God who wants to transform your life. The God who wants to make that brand-new creature out of you!

These are God's personal love letters to you. Did you ever get a love letter from your husband or wife before you were married? Did you throw it in a corner and say, "I don't have time to read that today—this week—this month. I'll get around to reading it some one of these times!"? Or did you do just like I did when I got love letters from Charles? I opened them up immediately and read them through once, then twice, then three times and sometimes more often than that. Before I met Charles, I opened up the checks for my printing company first of all, but when those love letters started coming from my beloved, I threw everything else aside to open them first.

We should feel the same way about God's Word! I wonder what excuse we're going to have when we stand before Him on that day of judgment and He says: "Did you read My love letters—all of them?" Think of some of the flimsy excuses some of us are going to have! "I was too busy . . . I always meant to, but just never found the time!" How is God going to feel when we say, "Well, just some of them because I could never understand the Old Testament"?

Let's pray, shall we?

Father, we thank You for Your Holy Word. Somehow right now, Father, Your presence is so real and so near and so dear as each one of us realizes that our own Bible is our personal love letter from You. Father, Tom and Patty's Bible, and Joan and Bob's Bible, doesn't have Charles and Frances; it has Tom and Patty, and Bob and Joan, so that's your special word just to them. Father, we thank You for the fact that You've given to each one of us a personal love letter. A love letter to take to heart, a love letter to read, reread and reread and reread. A love letter where we can just wallow in Your love, as we realize that You're just talking to us and not to anyone else in the entire world. Father, we love You, we worship You, we bow down before You—bow down before You, because You've given us such a simple, easy plan to follow, because all we have to do is read Your Word and know what You say to us, and that's the answer to it all. That's the way to the abundant life.

Father, we pray right now that every person in this moment of prayer will just somehow lift up whatever need they have. Jesus, we just ask You to reach down and take every need out of every hand because we've never known anybody to reach up where You didn't reach down, and answer their prayer. We just thank You for what You're doing in hearts right now. Lord Jesus, if there are those who need to make a new decision to serve You and give their life to You, let them cry out right now in silence saying, "Jesus, it's all the way with me from now on!"

Father, if there are those reading these pages who have unconfessed sin in their lives, may they, in the holiness of Your Presence in these pages, confess that sin right now and say "Lord Jesus, forgive me."

Father, may each of us who have read this chapter have a renewed determination to spend more time in Your love letters. Thank You for loving us. I often wonder why You do, but I'm not questioning it. I'm just going to accept Your love and say "Thank You, Jesus. Thank You, Jesus. Thank You, Jesus, that You did all of this just for me," just like every person reading this book can say "just for me." Thank You for what you're doing in the heart of every person who reads this book.

EPHESIANS

Ephesians 1:4-8

"Long ago, even before he made the world, God chose us to be his very own, through what Christ would do for us; he decided then to make us holy in his eyes, without a single fault—we who stand before him covered with his love. His unchanging plan has always been to adopt us into his own family by sending Jesus Christ to die for us. And he did this because he wanted to!

"Now all praise to God for his wonderful kindness to us and his favor that he has poured out upon us, because we belong to his dearly loved Son. So overflowing is his kindness towards us that he took away all our sins through the blood of his Son, by whom we are saved; and he has showered down upon us the richness of his grace—for how well he understands us and knows what is best for us at all times."

I often refer to Ephesians as the "wow" book of the Bible. The promises in this book are really earthshaking and almost beyond the scope of the human mind to understand. There is some tremendous advice throughout on how to live the Christian life. God always does His part, but there are many areas of our life where He always gives us the choice of doing what He wants us to do, or following our own natural desires. Somehow if we understand what God expects us to do, and if we understand how He expects us to live, it makes it much easier all the way around. We don't have problems trying to live as God wants us to, as long as we KNOW what it is He wants, and He doesn't have problems with us when we are trying to be the kind of a person He wants us to be.

Look at what this part of Ephesians has to say concerning you. Since my Bible is personal all the way throughout, I want to let you see what it says: "God chose Frances to be his very own, through what Christ would do for her; he decided then to make her holy in his eyes, without a single fault—Frances, who stands before him covered with his love." (Put your own name in there and see what it does to you when you read it out loud, right now!)

That is almost beyond the capabilities of my finite mind to understand that God in His love and His grace and His mercy was willing to choose me, and to make me holy in His eyes, without a single fault, and today I stand before Him covered with His love. At this point I am saying this about myself because of what that verse does for me, and I know at this moment it must be doing exactly the same thing for you when you realize the magnitude of this beautiful promise of God.

Read on. "His unchanging plan has always been to adopt Frances into his own family by sending Jesus Christ to die for her. *And he did this because he wanted to!*" Just think, in His beautiful plan to adopt you and me into His own family, He let Jesus die for us because He wanted to. Not because He had to, but because He wanted to.

Read on in verse 7. "So overflowing is his kindness towards Frances that he took away all her sins through the blood of his Son, by whom Frances is saved." How can we possibly understand the fullness of His love and kindness toward us when He removed all of our sins through the blood of Jesus! Did you ever try to total up all the things that have ever been sin in your life, and then be aware of the fact that God took them all away? All I have to do is even think of a few of the things He's done for me in the way of forgiveness, and I know it would take me more than a hundred years to even attempt to write down all the things He's forgiven me for. Hallelujah! And yet all you and I have to do is to accept it. And this promise assures you that you are adopted into His own family. You're not a stepchild, you're a real part of His family, just like Jesus.

. . . Now keep reading on: "And he has showered down upon Frances the richness of his grace—for how well he understands Frances and knows what is best for Frances at all times."

Isn't it beautiful to know because of His kindness He has showered down upon me (and you, too) the very richness of His grace and His grace will lift you above the things of this world. Isn't it exciting to know how well He understands you (and me, too) and isn't it beyond one's ability to describe to have the promise that He knows what is best for me (and you) at all times? Haven't you ever wondered what would be the best thing for you? And then haven't you shilly-shallied back and forth trying to make up your mind. It's beautiful to know that He knows what is best for me at all times, and all I've got to do is to walk with Him moment by moment and the best is always mine. Not because I'm smart at all, not because I'm a favorite at all, but because His Word says so! Hallelujah!

Ephesians 1:9-12

"God has told us his secret reason for sending Christ, a plan he decided on in mercy long ago; and this was his purpose: that when the time is ripe he will gather us all together from wherever we are—in heaven or on earth—to be with him in Christ, forever. Moreover, because of what Christ has done we have become gifts to God that he delights in, for as part of God's sovereign plan we were chosen from the beginning to be his, and all things happen just as he decided long ago. God's purpose in this was that we should praise God and give glory to him for doing these mighty things for us, who were the first to trust in Christ."

Did you ever wonder what God's reason was for sending Christ? His purpose was "that when the time is ripe he will gather us all together from wherever we are—in heaven or on earth—to be with him in Christ, FOREVER." Forever, forever, forever, forever, forever. No more night or day, no more time to worry about, no nothing, just the privilege of being with Him in heaven.

Did you ever realize that God's Word says (and so it's a promise) that you become GIFTS to God that He delights in? I can't think of anything about me that God might want as a gift, and yet His Word says when I make it personal that "because of what Christ has done Frances has become a gift to God that He delights in" . . . God, please don't throw any of Your gifts away, even though they may not be all that You want. But thank You, Lord, that You delight in this old gift of my life.

What was God's purpose in all this? Look what His Word says: "God's purpose in this was that we should *praise* God and give *glory* to him for doing these mighty things for us, who were the first to trust in Christ."

Father, we praise You, we magnify You, we give You the honor and the glory. We thank You, Father, that You allowed us to become gifts that You could delight in. Father, may we never run short of praise to tell You how much we love You, and may we never shortcut You on time to praise You and worship You and give You the glory for doing these mighty things for us.

Father, we love You!

Ephesians 1:13-14

"And because of what Christ did, all you
others too, who heard the Good News about how
to be saved, and trusted Christ, were marked as
belonging to Christ by the Holy Spirit, who long
ago had been promised to all of us Christians. His
presence within us is God's guarantee that he really
will give us all that he promised; and the Spirit's
seal upon us means that God has already purchased
us and that he guarantees to bring us to himself.
This is just one more reason for us to praise our
glorious God."

Father, that verse just says it so specifically that the
presence of the Holy Spirit within us is Your guarantee that
He will give us all that You promised and that promise
includes bringing us to Yourself.

Just one more reason for us to praise You. We praise
You, Father, we love You, Father, we worship You, we adore
You. We praise You for Your goodness to us, we praise You
for Your promises. We praise You because Your Word comes
so alive when quickened by the Holy Spirit. We praise You
because You gave us the Holy Spirit to make Your Scriptures
come alive, so that we might know all the things You have in
store for us.

Ephesians 1:15-18

"That is why, ever since I heard of your
strong faith in the Lord Jesus and of the love you
have for Christians everywhere, I have never
stopped thanking God for you. I pray for you
constantly, asking God, the glorious Father of our

Lord Jesus Christ, to give you wisdom to see
clearly and really understand who Christ is and all
that he has done for you. I pray that your hearts
will be flooded with light so that you can see
something of the future he has called you to share.
I want you to realize that God has been made rich
because we who are Christ's have been given to
him!"

Listen to this beautiful promise of God. This is one
verse I don't understand, and probably never will, but that's
unimportant. I just accept it. Do you realize that God has
been made rich because you who belong to Christ have been
given to Him? All I could think of was, "God, how could
You be made rich because of me?" There sure isn't any good
reason, except the only reason that's important. His Word
says so, and if His Word says He is rich because I have been
given to Him, then I shall be eternally grateful, even though
I am not capable of understanding His mercy; I just accept
it.

Father, thank You, that because I belong to Jesus I have
been given to You and that You have been made rich because
of this. Father, nothing about me could make You rich,
except Your promise, and what a joy it is, Father, to know
that in some little way You have been made rich because of
me. I am so rich because of You and what You have done for
my life, and I thank You for it.

Ephesians 2:1-6

"Once you were under God's curse, doomed
forever for your sins. You went along with the
crowd and were just like all the others, full of sin,
obeying Satan, the mighty prince of the power of
the air, who is at work right now in the hearts of
those who are against the Lord. All of us used to

be just as they are, our lives expressing the evil within us, doing every wicked thing that our passions or our evil thoughts might lead us into. We started out bad, being born with evil natures, and were under God's anger just like everyone else.

"But God is so rich in mercy; he loved us so much that even though we were spiritually dead and doomed by our sins, he gave us back our lives again when he raised Christ from the dead—only by his undeserved favor have we ever been saved—and lifted us up from the grave into glory along with Christ, where we sit with him in the heavenly realms—all because of what Christ Jesus did."

This verse brings a chuckle to my mind because once in a while we forget what we were before we met Jesus. Not everyone has the same background, but we are all sinners of one kind or another, and I don't really believe in God's eyes one sin is worse than another, do you? And so, while some people are wicked in the world's eyes because they drink and smoke and carouse around, others are equally wicked in God's eyes because of their critical attitude, or their inability to tell the truth, or many other little "Christian" sins. The Bible says we all started out the same; praise God, He has no favorites.

Now read verses 4 on, and see the reason why we can rejoice even though we were once under God's curse. "But God is so rich in mercy; he loved Frances so much that even though she was spiritually dead and doomed by her sins, he gave her back her life again when he raised Christ from the dead—only by his undeserved favor has Frances ever been saved—and lifted Frances up from the grave into glory along with Christ, where she sits with him in the heavenly realms—all because of what Christ Jesus did."

How true that promise of God is. I was so spiritually dead and doomed by my own sins, and yet His mercy was so rich and so great that He gave me life again because of Jesus! And to think that He has lifted me up from the spiritual grave into glory along with Christ, where I sit in the heavenly realms. And even though I am "in" the world, I am not "of" the world, so I sit in the heavenly realms day by day. Hallelujah! Your name goes in there just as beautifully as mine does, so see what it says to you? Did He raise you from spiritual deadness and up into glory along with Christ? Hallelujah! Whoever thought life could be this fabulous?

Ephesians 3:17-21

> "And I pray that Christ will be more and more at home in your hearts, living within you as you trust in him. May your roots go down deep into the soil of God's marvelous love; and may you be able to feel and understand, as all God's children should, how long, how wide, how deep, and how high his love really is; and to experience this love for yourselves, though it is so great that you will never see the end of it or fully know or understand it. And so at last you will be filled up with God himself.
>
> "Now glory be to God who by his mighty power at work within us is able to do far more than we would ever dare to ask or even dream of—infinitely beyond our highest prayers, desires, thoughts, or hopes. May he be given glory forever and ever through endless ages because of his master plan of salvation for the church through Jesus Christ."

This portion of Ephesians might possibly be my favorite passage in the Bible because there are so many glorious promises of God contained in these few verses. The first time I ever read it, I wrote "WOW" alongside of it. That's just how I felt!

Read the first one, personalized: "And I pray that Christ will be more and more at home in Frances' heart, living *within* her as she trusts in him."

One of the first things that God said to me through His Holy Word was that He wanted to live IN and THROUGH me. He said: "I don't want YOU to try because nobody can live the Christian life." He said, "I want to live in and through you. I want to do MY work in and through YOU. I don't want you to do it because you're not capable of it." Then He simply said, "Would you just get yourself out of the way, and give Me YOU, and let Me have your body to speak in and through."

Why God should want to live in and through such an imperfect vessel as I am, I'll never know, but praise God, I don't have to know! I just have to believe, because His Word says so!!!

Now keep on reading and see that next beautiful promise coming up! "May your roots go down deep into the soil of God's marvelous love; and may you be able to feel and understand, as all God's children should, how long, how wide, how deep, and how high his love really is; and to experience this love for yourselves, though it is so great that you will never see the end of it or fully know or understand it. (Now listen to God's promise for YOU!) And so at last FRANCES will be filled up with God himself!"

The first time I ever put my name in that Scripture, I found it impossible to comprehend that the God who created the universe, the God who hung the stars in place, the God who is all in all, had promised that someday I would be filled all the way up to the top with Himself. Just sit for a moment, will you, as you read this, and meditate on what that says to you! God says that someday YOU will be filled all the way up to the top with His glorious presence. Who could ever ask for anything more?

Read on . . . "Now glory be to God who by his mighty power at work within Frances is able to do far more than

Frances would ever dare to ask or even dream of—infinitely beyond her highest prayers, desires, thoughts, or hopes."

See how the Word of God emphasizes again that it's God working WITHIN you that makes the difference. I think at this moment of the crippled little boy with cerebral palsy that I held in my arms and cried out to God to heal him. Nothing I ever did would have healed him, but, "God, who by his mighty power at work within Frances" did! And so God "is able to do far more than Frances would ever dare to ask or even dream of—infinitely beyond her highest prayers, desires, thoughts, or hopes."

Thank You, Jesus! Thank You, Jesus! May He be given glory forever and ever through endless ages because of His master plan of salvation for the church through Jesus Christ!

Ephesians 4:23-32

"Now your attitudes and thoughts must all be constantly changing for the better. Yes, you must be a new and different person, holy and good. Clothe yourself with this new nature.

"Stop lying to each other; tell the truth, for we are parts of each other and when we lie to each other we are hurting ourselves. If you are angry, don't sin by nursing your grudge. Don't let the sun go down with you still angry—get over it quickly; for when you are angry you give a mighty foothold to the devil.

"If anyone is stealing he must stop it and begin using those hands of his for honest work so he can give to others in need. Don't use bad language. Say only what is good and helpful to those you are talking to, and what will give them a blessing.

"Don't cause the Holy Spirit sorrow by the way you live. Remember, he is the one who marks you to be present on that day when salvation from sin will be complete.

"Stop being mean, bad-tempered and angry. Quarreling, harsh words, and dislike of others should have no place in your lives. Instead, be kind to each other, tender-hearted, forgiving one another, just as God has forgiven you because you belong to Christ."

Here's something that can really change your life-style. This little section has revised and revamped the lives of many people who realize that what seems to some to be a simple statement, is really a promise. "Now your attitudes and thoughts must ALL be changing for the better. Yes, you must be a new and different person, holy and good. Clothe yourself with this new nature."

Do you realize what this says? It says to me when I first became a Christian (and still does) that Jesus would give me the power to be able to change all of my attitudes. The selfishness had to go and the critical thoughts I had about people had to be changing for the better, because Jesus said so. And if He said so, then He would give me the power to see that the attitudes and thoughts were changing. And see His next promise. "Yes, you must be a new and different person, holy and good." He didn't say I could go on being the same old person, with a critical spirit, with a filthy mouth, with a lot of sin continuing in my life. He said very emphatically that I must be a "new and different person, holy and good." How could I be holy and good? There wasn't any way, except He promised that I had to be, so it was His power that would give me the ability to be what He wanted me to be. And then He went on to say, "Clothe yourself with this new nature." He didn't say to just put on one stocking of this nature, and leave the other old clothes on; He didn't say just to put on a new blouse and leave the rest of the clothes the same, He said to "clothe" myself with this new nature, which meant removing all of the "old" self and covering it with the new. Hallelujah!

Now look how personal He gets and how He gets into that inner man of you. "Frances and Mary, stop lying to each other; tell the truth, for we are parts of each other and when we lie to each other we are hurting ourselves." Did it ever dawn on you how many Christians fail to be truthful? Many of them think it's all right to tell a little "white" lie. If we really believed God's Word, we would know that when we lie to each other we are hurting OURSELVES! Did you ever think about it that way? Did you ever think that when you speed a "little" over the limit, the one you are hurting is yourself? You're not hurting the police officer who is sent there to protect you, you are hurting yourself, and who wants to hurt themselves? Not me!

Would you like to conduct a little survey? Try for the next 30 days to be 100 percent truthful in all situations, and if you aren't quite 100 percent, write it down on a little scratch pad, and see how many times during the week you are checked by the Holy Spirit. This can be one of the most interesting experiments in the world. Be sure and put your name in these verses, too! We don't only put our names in the "good" places, but in the "bad" places also. Do you know that some of your greatest Christian growth can come when God is stepping all over your toes?

As long as we've started, we might as well go on letting the Holy Spirit step on our toes. "Frances, if you are angry, don't sin by nursing your grudge. Frances, don't let the sun go down with you still angry—get over it quickly; for when you are angry you give a mighty foothold to the devil."

How many times have married couples turned their backs on each other when they go to bed because one or the other is "miffed" because of something the other one said, or because of some misunderstanding. This is one of the greatest tricks of the devil himself, because when you let anger stay in you, he really gets a mighty foothold!

Did you ever start to get over being mad, and then just by thinking about it *(I'll make him suffer),* decided you were going to stay mad? This is when Satan really has a field day, because as long as he can keep you thinking about how mad you are, he can keep your mind off the things of God! Just try thinking about God's love when you're mad at someone! Can't be done!

God's Word is so explicit in this matter, let's forget all about ever getting mad, shall we?

Let's continue, if you still have courage. "If anyone is stealing he must stop it and begin using those hands of his for honest work so he can give to others in need." Now you might be saying, "I'm honest, I wouldn't steal a single, solitary thing." Let's think about that a little more, shall we? Do you work? Do you conscientiously give your employer the full eight hours daily that he pays you for, or do you spend time about the water cooler or drinking fountain? How much time do you spend on coffee breaks . . . how much time do you waste drinking Cokes and the like (even if they're at your desk) . . . how much time do you spend "visiting" in the office? Ask yourself: "If I'm getting paid for this time, am I totally honest when I waste this much time doing things that are not productive for my employer?" It's amazing how much more efficient we can be when we think about it this way.

You may not have courage for this next part, but I hope you will hang in here with me, because it can really bless your life. (Remember God had to step all over me or I wouldn't have discovered this myself, and it really hurt!) "Don't use bad language. Say only what is good and helpful to those you are talking to, and what will give them a blessing."

You're saying right now, "I don't use bad language. I have never sworn or cursed or used bad language." It just depends on what you call bad language. Do you know that "bad" language can be almost anything you say, depending on your attitude when you say it? Did you know that a lot of Christians get involved in what Charles describes as "shoot cussing" in his book? How many times have you said, "Oh my goodness!" knowing full well that your goodness is as filthy rags. Anyone with a critical spirit can be using "bad" language when they criticize another. Remember when you criticize anyone to a third party, you are not blessing them at all! Look what the Bible says: "Frances, say only what is good and helpful to those who you are talking to, and what will give them a blessing!"

This is one of the places where making the Bible personal can really hurt, but one of the greatest blessings that can ever occur to you will occur during these moments of hurt. (Think how good it's going to be when you've dropped that nasty habit.) Hallelujah!!!

Skip down just a little bit more, will you? "Stop being mean, bad-tempered and angry. Quarreling, harsh words, and dislike of others should have no place in your lives. Instead, be kind to each other, tender-hearted, forgiving one another, just as God has forgiven you because you belong to Christ."

Have you ever said, "I can't help it, I was just made this way"? Great, if you want to go on believing that way. But did you know that when you've been born again you are a brand-new creature in Christ, and don't have a right any longer to have been "born" *that way*, because you sure haven't been "born again" that way?

Think how easy it is to be tender-hearted, forgiving one another just because of the way God forgave you because you belong to Christ!

Glory, God, You make it so easy.

Ephesians 5:1-11

"Follow God's example in everything you do just as a much loved child imitates his father. Be full of love for others, following the example of

Christ who loved you and gave himself to God as a sacrifice to take away your sins. And God was pleased, for Christ's love for you was like sweet perfume to him.

"Let there be no sex sin, impurity or greed among you. Let no one be able to accuse you of any such things. Dirty stories, foul talk and coarse jokes—these are not for you. Instead, remind each other of God's goodness and be thankful.

"You can be sure of this: The kingdom of Christ and of God will never belong to anyone who is impure or greedy, for a greedy person is really an idol worshiper—he loves and worships the good things of this life more than God. Don't be fooled by those who try to excuse these sins, for the terrible wrath of God is upon all those who do them. Don't even associate with such people. For though once your heart was full of darkness, now it is full of light from the Lord, and your behavior should show it! Because of this light within you, you should do only what is good and right and true.

"Learn as you go along what pleases the Lord. Take no part in the worthless pleasures of evil and darkness, but instead, rebuke and expose them."

I think of my little grandson, David, who loves his daddy so much he follows him all over the place, and imitates everything he does. If Tom laughs, he laughs. If Tom stamps his foot, David stamps his foot! If Tom hugs him, David hugs him right back. He does his very best to imitate everything that his daddy does. Why? Because he really loves his daddy! And we should be exactly the same way about God. We don't have to worry about how to behave because He just tells us to behave and follow His example. "Be full of love for others." God is so plain in His Word about loving our neighbors, and loving others more than we love ourselves. If we believe that Christ lives in us, we should always be bubbling over with love.

Then He tells you what not to do. And He makes it so simple, and when you come right down to it, God is not trying to bind you into a miserable life, He is just freeing you from doing the things that really never made you happy. I think of all the dirty jokes I told before I met Jesus. I think of the swear words I knew and used before I met Jesus. They really didn't make me happy, it was just a cover-up for a need in my life. When Jesus met the need, there was no place for this type of thing, and praise God! I don't believe I could remember a dirty joke if I tried. (And I'm not going to try!) Thank You, Jesus, for Your cleansing power!

I just love the eighth, ninth, and tenth verses in a real special way because He firmly promises that now it is "full of light from the Lord, and your behavior should show it!" Now that He's promised that your heart is full of light from the Lord, who could help but show it! And now another promise where He says that because of this light within you, you're going to change. You just can't help it. Make it personal, and see what it says: "Because of this light within Frances, Frances should do only what is good and right and true." Isn't it easy, because He tells you because of this light you'll have the power to do only those things that are good and right and true?

He continues on to say that you should learn as you go along to please Him. In other words, get into His Word and find out what pleases Him. And then He gives a clear instruction concerning sin: "Take no part in the worthless pleasures of evil and darkness, Frances, but instead, rebuke and expose them." He certainly makes it plain about staying away from sin; and He lets you know what sin is, just so you won't have to debate in your mind whether it's sin or not. A good rule to follow is, "When in doubt, leave it out."

Occasionally I've heard people say that this type of verse isn't really good to read, but I often think God's instructions are so simple, they make His promises easy to understand when they're obeyed!

Thank You, Jesus, for never leaving us in doubt as to what's right and what's wrong!

Ephesians 5:21-33

"Honor Christ by submitting to each other. You wives must submit to your husbands' leadership in the same way you submit to the Lord. For a husband is in charge of his wife in the same way Christ is in charge of his body the church. (He gave his very life to take care of it and be its Savior!) So you wives must willingly obey your husbands in everything, just as the church obeys Christ.

"And you husbands, show the same kind of love to your wives as Christ showed to the church when he died for her, to make her holy and clean, washed by baptism and God's Word; so that he could give her to himself as a glorious church without a single spot or wrinkle or any other blemish, being holy and without a single fault. That is how husbands should treat their wives, loving them as parts of themselves. For since a man and his wife are now one, a man is really doing himself a favor and loving himself when he loves his wife! No one hates his own body but lovingly cares for it, just as Christ cares for his body the church, of which we are parts.

"(That the husband and wife are one body is proved by the Scripture which says, 'A man must leave his father and mother when he marries, so that he can be perfectly joined to his wife, and the two shall be one.') I know this is hard to understand, but it is an illustration of the way we are parts of the body of Christ.

"So again I say, a man must love his wife as a part of himself; and the wife must see to it that she deeply respects her husband—obeying, praising and honoring him."

I love everything the Bible has to say about marriage! God certainly knew what He was doing when He made man and woman, and He knew what He was doing when He laid down the ground rules! Again, I feel if we would make all of God's Word personal, it would speak to us in a much greater way! With no comments, I'm going to put down what my Bible says and I think it will speak by itself.

"Honor Christ by submitting to each other. Frances must submit to Charles' leadership in the same way Frances submits to the Lord. For Charles is in charge of Frances in the same way Christ is in charge of his body the church. (He gave his very life to take care of it and be its Savior!) So Frances must willingly obey Charles in everything, just as the church obeys Christ.

"And Charles, show the same kind of love to Frances as Christ showed to the church when he died for her, to make her holy and clean, washed by baptism and God's Word; so that he could give her to himself as a glorious church without a single spot or wrinkle or any other blemish, being holy and without a single fault. That is how Charles should treat Frances, loving Frances as part of Charles. For since Charles and Frances are now one, Charles is really doing himself a favor and loving himself when he loves Frances. No one hates his own body but lovingly cares for it, just as Christ cares for his body, the church, of which we are parts.

"(That Charles and Frances are one body is proved by the Scripture which says, 'Charles must leave his father and mother when he marries, so that he can be perfectly joined to Frances, and the two shall be one.') I know this is hard to understand, but it is an illustration of the way we are parts of the body of Christ.

"So again I say, Charles must love Frances as a part of himself, and Frances must see to it that she deeply respects Charles—obeying, praising and honoring him."

Hallelujah! Thank You, Jesus, for making it so plain how married people should love each other. I want to encourage every married couple to put their names in this beautiful part of God's Word, and see what it does to their marriage. This is the way our house is run and this is why we believe our marriage is perfect! Just simply because of God's Word, not because of either of us!

COLOSSIANS

The book of Colossians is one of the most exciting books in the Bible . . . or at least that's the way it appears to me. Many of the truths of the real secret of Christian living are plainly, yet gloriously, stated in this beautiful book. My first inclination was to just quote the entire book, but then it seemed best to pull out the most spectacular parts for help in our daily walk with Jesus.

Colossians 1:11-12

"We are praying, too, that you will be filled with his mighty, glorious strength so that you can keep going no matter what happens—always full of the joy of the Lord, and always thankful to the Father who has made us fit to share all the wonderful things that belong to those who live in the kingdom of light."

What a great promise of God that you will be filled with His mighty, glorious strength so that you can *keep going, no matter what happens* . . . and always full of the joy of the Lord. Isn't it satisfying to know that there is a *power* that is sufficient to keep you going regardless of what comes along? And we can ALWAYS be full of the Joy of the Lord. No place in God's Holy Word for long-face Christians. Hallelujah!

Colossians 1:15-17

"Christ is the exact likeness of the unseen God. He existed before God made anything at all, and, in fact, Christ himself is the Creator who made everything in heaven and earth, the things we can see and the things we can't; the spirit world with its kings and kingdoms, its rulers and authorities; all were made by Christ for his own use and glory. He was before all else began and it is his power that holds everything together."

I hope you're reading each and every one of these passages of Scripture carefully and slowly, meditating on what God is saying to YOU, right now through these words. Christ Himself is the Creator who made everything in heaven and earth, and look at these words, "It is his power that holds everything together." Are you really aware of the fact that this power is an awesome thing? When the end of the world comes, nobody is going to have to destroy the earth. All Christ has to do is to let go and there it is—BOOM! and it exists no more.

Cup your fingers together like you're holding a round ball in between your two hands, letting your fingertips lightly touch each other. Just imagine you're holding the entire world in your hands—now just separate your fingers and hands—that's all Christ has to do to withdraw His holding power on the earth and the earth will just disintegrate. Your own body would just fly into pieces because there would be nothing to hold it together when Christ withdraws His power.

How fabulous to know you serve a living Jesus with that much strength!

Colossians 1:20-23

"It was through what his Son did that God cleared a path for everything to come to him—all things in heaven and on earth—for Christ's death on the cross has made peace with God for all by his blood. This includes you who were once so far away from God. You were his enemies and hated him and were separated from him by your evil thoughts and actions, yet now he has brought you back as his friends. He has done this through the death on the cross of his own human body, and now as a result Christ has brought you into the very presence of God, and you are standing there before him with nothing left against you—nothing left that he could even chide you for; the only condition is that you fully believe the Truth, standing in it steadfast and firm, strong in the Lord, convinced of the Good News that Jesus died for you, and never shifting from trusting him to save you. This is the wonderful news that came to each of you and is now spreading all over the world. And I, Paul, have the joy of telling it to others."

Read those first two lines. In spite of all of our fumbling around and messing up things God cleared a path for everything to come to Him, for Christ's death on the cross has made peace with God for all by His blood. Regardless of what your sin might have been, Christ's death on the cross has declared peace with God—for some? No, for ALL by His blood. And then look and see what He did immediately following that. Picture in your own mind that because of this Christ has brought you (regardless of what you've done) into the very presence of God, and you are standing there before Him with NOTHING left against you—nothing that He could even chide you for.

Read that again slowly and see what it really says. You are in the very presence of the almighty God, with absolutely nothing of your old sins left against you . . . nothing of your past . . . you are standing absolutely naked before Him because you have nothing to hide, because there isn't a single solitary thing that He could even chide you for because Jesus' blood on the cross took care of every single thing you've ever done. I don't believe I've ever read this particular verse of Scripture without almost physically feeling that I've been lifted right into the presence of God. Hallelujah!

Like all of God's promises, however, there is a condition, and the condition to this one is a strict one, but an exciting one, because it's the only way you'll ever know the abundant life. "The only condition is that you fully believe the Truth, standing in it steadfast and firm, strong in the Lord, convinced of the Good News that Jesus died for you, and *never shifting* from trusting him to save you." The secret of that little part of the verse is the words "never shifting." The sand shifts—you've seen it blow in the wind and completely disappear. The Christian is to be so founded in the Word of God that he never shifts—he stands on the rock of Jesus and doesn't waver back and forth.

Now finish off this little section with the last sentence, making it personal, of course. "And I, Frances, have the joy of telling it to others." And so do you. God said so, if you'll just put your own name in there.

What a privilege to be able to have the joy of telling the Good News to others!

Colossians 1:26-27

"He has kept this secret for centuries and
generations past, but now at last it has pleased him
to tell it to those who love him and live for him,
and the riches and glory of his plan are for you .

Gentiles too. And this is the secret: that Christ in your hearts is your only hope of glory."

I'm going to ask you to read this particular part in the *King James* version. "Christ in you, the hope of glory." Read it with the emphasis on the word "in." "Christ IN you, the hope of glory."

I have often been surprised to find that many people who have walked the Christian road for years, and who have struggled for victory, have never discovered this very simple secret to the successful Christian life: that Christ lives *in* you—not around you—not up in heaven, but actually living *in and through you* as He does His work in a body today called Charles, or Frances, or May or Bob or Joan, or Susie or Harold, or whatever your name is. The secret of being born again is to *know* that you *know* that you *know* that Jesus Christ is living IN you. The minute you discover this, you have the hope of glory and victorious life, because the life you are living is no longer your own—it belongs to Jesus, because He is living in and through you.

Right now I want you to do something special. I want you to put your hand over your heart and feel your heartbeat! Are you aware of the fact that if you are truly born again, the heartbeat that you feel is not your own, but the heartbeat of Jesus Christ as He lives in and through you! I never feel my own heartbeat without being reminded of the Person who is living in and through that very heartbeat.

Colossians 1:28-29

"So everywhere we go we talk about Christ to all who will listen, warning them and teaching them as well as we know how. We want to be able to present each one to God, perfect because of what Christ has done for each of them. This is my work, and I can do it only because Christ's mighty energy is at work within me."

The greatest privileges in the world are given to the Christians who will believe what God's Word says and will make it apply to their own personal lives. Look at what making the above verse personal does to the Scripture. Paul wasn't only talking about his own life. When you believe the Scriptures were written for you TODAY and you put your own name in them, you can see you have a responsibility." So everywhere Charles and I go we talk about Christ to all. . . . This is our work, and Charles and I can do it only because of Christ's mighty energy . . . at work within us."

Do you really talk about Christ to all who will listen, or do you shirk this responsibility? Do you warn people and teach people *as well as you know how?* Do you have this burning desire to be able to present each one to God, perfect because of what Christ has done for each of them? So many times we don't talk about Jesus because we don't realize what He has done, not only for us, but for the world out there that doesn't know Him.

Charles and I love the end of this verse because it gives the only way we can do it. We often think about the schedule we maintain, and the physical strain it is on us, and yet somehow or other, we always seem to make it and have all the energy we need to do what God has called us to do. Why? Only one reason! This is *our* work, and we can only do it because of Christ's mighty energy at work within us. If we didn't have the supernatural power of Christ's mighty energy at work within us, we'd have collapsed many times from exhaustion. But praise God! We have a promise to stand on in God's Word.

Thank You, Jesus!

Colossians 2:2

"For God's secret plan, now at last made known, is Christ himself. In him lie hidden all the mighty, untapped treasures of wisdom and knowledge."

What is God's secret plan? Christ Himself. Think beyond these few little words and let your imagination expand to understand what this really means, and then go to verse 3 and see the magnitude of who Jesus Christ really is. Where do all the mighty, untapped treasures of wisdom and knowledge lie? Right in Him. Everything that has ever been done, is ever done, or ever will be done will be because of the wisdom and knowledge of Jesus Christ as He apportions it out in various ways. All the space inventions were known to Jesus Christ before the world ever began; all of the so-called marvels of this age come from the mighty, untapped treasures of wisdom and knowledge which are possessed by Jesus Christ.

In conjunction with this promise, I love what it says over in James 1:5: "If you want to know what God wants you to do, ask him, and he will gladly tell you, for he is always ready to give a bountiful supply of wisdom to all who ask him; he will not resent it." Think what that really means— whenever you lack wisdom, just ask God because it says He will not just tell you, but will tell you gladly, and He will not resent it.

Not only do all the untapped treasures of wisdom lie in Jesus Christ, they are available to all who will ask! How much more could you want?

Colossians 2:6-10

"And now just as you trusted Christ to save you, trust him, too, for each day's problems; live in vital union with him. Let your roots grow down into him and draw up nourishment from him. See that you go on growing in the Lord, and become strong and vigorous in the truth you were taught. Let your lives overflow with joy and thanksgiving for all he has done.

"Don't let others spoil your faith and joy with their philosophies, their wrong and shallow answers built on men's thoughts and ideas, instead of on what Christ has said. For in Christ there is all of God in a human body; *so you have everything when you have Christ,* and you are filled with God through your union with Christ. He is the highest Ruler, with authority over every other power."

This is one of the most glorious passages in the entire Bible! It gives so much in such a few words. But then, all of the Bible does the same thing. It gives you so much so fast!

We'll take it almost phrase by phrase, or sentence by sentence. Just apply each one to your own life. "And now just as you trusted Christ to save you, trust him, too, for *each day's problems;* live in vital union with him." Isn't it easy to trust Christ to save you? But then doesn't it end up hard to use that simple childlike faith that it took to make you a Christian to walk the daily Christian life? That's the secret—trust Him, not only for the BIG things in life, but for every single thing in life itself.

"Let your roots grow down into him and draw up nourishment from him. See that you go on growing in the Lord, and become strong and vigorous in the truth you were taught." Christianity is not just an experience of being born again, or "saved," because it is the same as any little plant you would put in the ground. If there is no soil from which to draw nourishment, the little plant will die. If the ground is full of weeds, its growth will be stunted and its very life will be choked out. If it's planted too shallow, it will die from the burning sun. The same thing is true of every Christian. Your roots must grow down into Him and draw up nourishment.

You can't just let them sprawl all over the place with thousands of other interests to feed your soul instead of drawing nourishment from Him. You have to continue "growing" so that you will become strong and vigorous. You can stop watering a plant and it will die. The same thing is true of the Christian life—you can keep it alive with watering it from the Word of God, or you can just let it wither, get sickly and die!

Then look what the Bible promises if you do these things. The very next sentence says: "Let your lives *overflow with joy* and thanksgiving for all he has done." Every single Christian should have a life that is overflowing with joy. Do you really believe that Jesus died for you? Do you really believe that He shed His blood on Calvary for your sins? Do you really? If you do, then you ought to be so full of the love of Jesus because of what He's done for you that you ought to literally be shouting all the time! Your lives ought to literally overflow at all times with joy and thanksgiving.

Now this doesn't mean that a Christian never has problems, because you're going to continue having problems. But what difference does it make how many problems when you've got the answer? When I went to school I made tremendous grades in math. I never cared how many problems were on the math test, because I had the answer! Now it might have been a different thing in history, because that was my most difficult subject, but do you know why? Only because I didn't have the answers! I heard someone say, "Jesus is the answer, what's your problem?" And isn't that really true? You can have all the problems in the world, but they'll never get you down as long as you remember that you really have the answer!

"Don't let others spoil your faith and joy with their philosophies, their wrong and shallow answers built on men's thoughts and ideas, instead of on what Christ has said." This meant a lot to me, because in the beginning stages of my Christian life there were many who said, "You'll get over it!

The novelty will wear off!" They didn't understand that something had really happened to me, that I was a new creature in Christ. Many people thought the tremendous enthusiasm I had when I met Jesus would pass away before long and would get old, but I fall more deeply in love with Him every year and I'm far more enthusiastic today than I was when I accepted Him as my Savior, because I really didn't have any idea of what He could or would do for me. Today I know there's so much more, and yet today I know so much more than I did when I asked Him to come into my heart. People told me I was too happy, so it couldn't be genuine; but the more I got into the Word of God, the more I discovered that there is joy, Joy, JOY, in the Christian life. Over and over Jesus mentions the fact that He came that our cup of JOY might overflow. The word joy appears in the Bible 164 times.

Verse 9 makes me absolutely feel an urge to fly straight up to heaven right now. "For in Christ there is all of God in a human body; *so you have everything when you have Christ,* and you are filled with God through your union with Christ. He is the highest Ruler, with authority over every other power."

How could we ever help but feel that we owned the whole world, when we actually do. Do you really believe that you have EVERYTHING when you have Christ? What a beautiful, mind-blowing thought! What joy, what peace, what contentment. If you believe the Bible is true, how could you help but stay on a mountaintop with this type of information given directly to you by God?

So many times we want to give the devil credit for a lot of things and forget the very last sentence of this group of verses. "He is the highest Ruler, with authority over every other power." WHO has authority over every other power? Does the devil? *Nope,* God's Word says that Christ is the highest Ruler, and He alone has authority over every other power.

God! . . . You are so good!

Colossians 3:2-3

"Let heaven fill your thoughts; don't spend your time worrying about things down here. You should have as little desire for this world as a dead person does. Your real life is in heaven with Christ and God."

I praise God for the church where I found Christ, because they taught me many things that I might not have learned someplace else. I also praise God for the pastor whom He used to bring me into a personal relationship with Jesus Christ, because one of the things I heard from the very start of my Christian experience was total commitment and holy living. There was a time when I might have thought that "holy" living was walking around with my hands folded looking pious (this wouldn't have appealed to me at all). But holy living is a life where you remain "in" the world, and yet are not a part of the world. I praise God that He removed from my heart the desire for the "things" of the world, and gave me an interest in only the things that pertain to His kingdom.

One time my son said, "Mother, you aren't any fun anymore, because you don't drink, smoke, dance, or tell dirty jokes!" And what happens so many times is people think you *give up* all these things for Jesus! I never gave up a single solitary thing. Christ just replaced all the worldly desires with a desire for the things of God. Who needs to smoke when you've got Jesus? There'll be no cigarettes in heaven . . . no pipes or chewing tobacco, either. Who needs to get "high" on martinis and the like when you can go much higher on God? Many times I've said I never quit drinking, I just changed fountains. Hallelujah! The fountain of life is far more satisfying to drink than anything else.

I heard someone once say, "I didn't give up dancing, I just changed partners," and that's a good way to express it, isn't it? Even as I am writing this today, I think about all the hours I spent dancing and try to remember why I thought it was fun. The places where I danced were too dim to see very well . . . too crowded to be comfortable, and too hot to enjoy . . . the music wasn't very conducive to joy in my soul; it was just escaping from the reality of the moment. Jesus so completely fills your life that you don't need these other things. Who needs to tell dirty jokes? There is so much joy in Jesus (because He promised it) that you don't need ANY of the things of the world!

Let's spend our time thinking about the things of God—it's much more exciting anyway. And why should we spend our time worrying? Because if we're trusting Jesus, there's no cause for worry.

And listen to what God's Word has to say in verse three. "You should have as little desire for this world as a dead person does. Your real life is in heaven with Christ and God." If you still have a desire for the things of this world, ask God to take them away, because His Word says your desires should be no more than those of a dead person, and a dead person sure can't have very many, can he? Your "real life is in heaven with Christ and God."

Praise God! the Bible makes it so simple . . . you don't need the things of the world, Jesus alone is all you need.

Colossians 3:17

"And whatever you do or say, let it be as a representative of the Lord Jesus, and come with him into the presence of God the Father to give him your thanks."

This is some of the most beautiful advice given in the Bible, if we will just take it to heart. Let everything that comes out of our mouth be said as a representative of the Lord Jesus. So many times, people who are Christians put their minds on the things of the carnal world and forget that everything we do or say should be as a representative of Jesus. Let the Spirit of God check you whenever you're saying things that might not be exactly what the Lord would have you say. This won't restrict you at all, even though you might think it does. It just guards you and keeps you from falling back into the traps of Satan. It is so true that a Christian has to be wary because Satan does rove around like a roaring lion seeking to devour us, and many times it's through just the little things we say, not realizing that we are playing right into Satan's hands.

Colossians 3:23-25

"Work hard and cheerfully at all you do, just as though you were working for the Lord and not merely for your masters, remembering that it is the Lord Christ who is going to pay you, giving you your full portion of all he owns. He is the one you are really working for. And if you don't do your best for him, he will pay you in a way that you won't like—for he has no special favorites who can get away with shirking."

In a world where we all have to work and make a living, we have a tendency to want to please our boss or the supervisor who is over us, and whose orders we have to follow. During the years I worked I always tried to please the various bosses because I knew if I did my job right I would more likely get an increase in pay. Men work all of their lives trying to be a success so they can make more money (more this year than they did last). Because we are tempted to measure success with how much of the material things of life we possess or can buy, yet what does God's Word say about who it is you are really working for? It says Jesus is the One you are *really* working for. And if you don't do your best for Him, He will pay you in a way that you won't like—for He has no special favorites who can get away with shirking. But listen to the promise there concerning the fact that He will give you a FULL portion of ALL He owns! Who is more generous than that?

Isn't that plain enough to let us know who our boss really is? And it is plain enough that you'll get paid in a way that you don't like, if you're not doing your best for Him. But just think of what He offers you when you do your best for Him. It's the best pay in the world, and remember that your final paycheck will come from Him, regardless of whom you have served during your lifetime—and the final one can either be real good or real bad, depending on what we've done with our lives.

ACTS

Acts 1:8

"But when the Holy Spirit has come upon you, you will receive power to testify about me with great effect, to the people in Jerusalem, throughout Judea, in Samaria, and to the ends of the earth, about my death and resurrection."

Acts 2:1-21

"Seven weeks had gone by since Jesus' death and resurrection, and the Day of Pentecost had now arrived. As the believers met together that day, suddenly there was a sound like the roaring of a mighty windstorm in the skies above them and it filled the house where they were meeting. Then, what looked like flames or tongues of fire appeared and settled on their heads. And everyone present was filled with the Holy Spirit and began speaking in languages they didn't know, for the Holy Spirit gave them this ability.

"Many godly Jews were in Jerusalem that day for the religious celebrations, having arrived from many nations. And when they heard the roaring in the sky above the house, crowds came running to see what it was all about, and were stunned to hear their own languages being spoken by the disciples.

" 'How can this be?' they exclaimed. 'For these men are all from Galilee, and yet we hear them speaking all the native languages of the lands where we were born! Here we are—Parthians, Medes, Elamites, men from Mesopotamia, Judea, Capadocia, Pontus, Ausia, Phrygia, Pamphylia, Egypt, the Cyrene language areas of Libya, visitors from Rome—both Jews and Jewish converts—Cretans, and Arabians. And we all hear these men telling in our own languages about the mighty miracles of God!'

"They stood there amazed and perplexed. 'What can this mean?' they asked each other.

"But others in the crowd were mocking. 'They're drunk, that's all!' they said.

"Then Peter stepped forward with the eleven apostles, and shouted to the crowd, 'Listen, all of you, visitors and residents of Jerusalem alike! Some of you are saying these men are drunk! It isn't true! It's much too early for that! People don't get drunk by 9 a.m.! No! What you see this morning was predicted centuries ago by the prophet Joel— "In the last days," God said, "I will pour out my Holy Spirit upon all mankind, and your sons and daughters shall prophesy, and your young men shall see visions, and your old men dream dreams. Yes, the Holy Spirit shall come upon all my servants, men and women alike, and they shall prophesy. And I will cause strange demonstrations in the heavens and on the earth—

blood and fire and clouds of smoke; the sun shall
turn black and the moon blood-red before that
awesome Day of the Lord arrives. But anyone who
asks for mercy from the Lord shall have it and shall
be saved." ' "

In my earliest stages of Christianity, I discovered the
book of Acts and loved the verses concerning the Power for
all things. I saw Jesus as the most powerful man that ever
lived, and after the Holy Spirit had come upon Him, He had
power to do all things! These two portions of God's Word tell
about His promise, and then His fulfillment of that promise
because He didn't leave us powerless!

I have often tried to visualize in my own mind what the
day of Pentecost must have been like. Can you imagine the
thoughts that would have run through your mind had you
been one of those 120? Seven long weeks had gone by, and
so far the promise that Jesus had given to His disciples had
not come true yet. I wonder if there might not have been a
little grumbling among some of them as to whether or not
the promised Holy Spirit would ever come. I wonder if some
of them might have even lost their faith a little, because so
much time had elapsed. I even wonder if some of them might
have panicked a little bit, wondering what was going to
happen to them if the Holy Spirit never came. I imagine some
of them were afraid they might go back into their old ways
without something to help them.

For those who still believed and had not doubted, I
imagine they had spent a lot of those seven weeks wondering
what the "Holy Spirit" was going to be like. I imagine they
visualized all kinds of things. Would it be something they
could eat like manna which would give them power? Would it
be something to drink which would give them power?

Sit there with them, will you, and imagine what you
might have thought the coming of the Holy Spirit would be
like. Would they be able to recognize the Holy Spirit? Would

this "Comforter" be a person, or what would it actually be? Would it be another man like Jesus who would be able to impart power into their lives? I have a feeling those who were waiting for the Holy Spirit probably had some of the most fearful moments of their lives between wondering if the Holy Spirit would ever come, and what it would be like when it came.

I have a feeling that none of them ever anticipated that there would suddenly be a sound like the roaring of a mighty windstorm in the skies. Can you imagine the tremendous noise that must have accompanied this supernatural demonstration? And can you imagine the fear which must have come upon all of them because of the unexpectedness of this moment? I wonder how many of them thought this was their last minute on earth—and wondered if this man Jesus had really told the truth when He spoke about eternal life, or . . . was this thing that was happening (whatever it was) going to be the thing that ended their lives, and maybe they would never know the truth.

Can you imagine the chaos that must have filled the Upper Room at that time? Can you imagine the thoughts that must have filled their minds when the tongues of fire appeared and began settling on their heads. Can you imagine what they thought when they saw the first tongue of fire appear—then another, then another, then another! I imagine that even though they might have wanted to run, they were glued to the spot. Somewhere in some of their wild thoughts somebody probably thought, "This is the 'hell' He was talking about, with the eternal fire." Wouldn't it be exciting to know what they really thought?

But really, that's unimportant. The important thing is to realize what happened to them when they were endued with Power from above. They immediately began to witness! They immediately took their light out from under a bushel and began to shine it around, so much to the extent that people thought they were drunk because they were speaking in all different languages.

Praise God! He sent us power to live the Christian life, and praise God! He has never withdrawn the Holy Spirit who is still here to empower us to live the Christian life and be witnesses for Him.

Verses with Impact from Acts

The entire book of Acts is a thrilling story, but I have tried to choose for you the verses that had the most terrific impact upon my life, and I hope that they will do the same thing for you!

I love all the stories about the miracles that Jesus did, and really love the Scriptures about what happened to the apostles after they received the Holy Spirit.

"Then Peter took the lame man by the hand and pulled him to his feet. And as he did, the man's feet and anklebones were healed and strengthened so that he came up with a leap, stood there a moment and began walking! Then, walking, leaping, and praising God, he went into the Temple with them."   *(Acts 3:7-8)*

"Jesus' name has healed this man—and you know how lame he was before. Faith in Jesus' name—faith given us from God—has caused this perfect healing."   *(Acts 3:16)*

"By what power, or by whose authority have you done this?"   *(Acts 4:7)*

". . . It was done in the name and power of Jesus from Nazareth, the Messiah, the man you crucified—but God raised back to life again. It is by his authority that this man stands here healed!"   *(Acts 4:10)*

"Meanwhile, the apostles were meeting regularly at the Temple in the area known as Solomon's Hall, and they did many remarkable miracles among the people."   *(Acts 5:12)*

"Sick people were brought out into the streets on beds and mats so that at least Peter's shadow would fall across some of them as he went by! And crowds came in from the Jerusalem suburbs, bringing their sick folk and those possessed by demons; and every one of them was healed."

(Acts 5:15)

"Stephen, the man so full of faith and the Holy Spirit's power, did spectacular miracles among the people."

(Acts 6:8)

"Crowds listened intently to what he (Philip) had to say because of the miracles he did. Many evil spirits were cast out, screaming as they left their victims, and many who were paralyzed or lame were healed, so there was much joy in the city." *(Acts 8:6-7)*

"Turning to the body he said, 'Get up, Dorcas,' and she opened her eyes! And when she saw Peter, she sat up! He gave her his hand and helped her up and called in the believers and widows, presenting her to them." (Dorcas was dead prior to this.) *(Acts 9:40)*

"While they were at Lystra, they came upon a man with crippled feet who had been that way from birth, so he had never walked. He was listening as Paul preached, and Paul noticed him and realized he had faith to be healed. So Paul called to him, 'Stand up!' and the man leaped to his feet and started walking!" *(Acts 14:8-9)*

"One day as we were going down to the place of prayer beside the river, we met a demon-possessed slave girl who was a fortune-teller, and earned much money for her masters. She followed along behind us shouting, 'These men are servants of God and they have come to tell you how to have your sins forgiven.'

"This went on day after day until Paul, in great distress, turned and spoke to the demon within her, 'I command you in the name of Jesus Christ to come out of her,' he said. And instantly it left her."   *(Acts 16:16-18)*

Think of the power given to these ordinary men by the Holy Spirit. Each of these acts required tremendous power—far more than any of them ever dreamed or hoped for—until the Holy Spirit came upon them. I love all the power promises in God's Word.

"And now, O Lord, hear their threats, and grant to your servants great boldness in their preaching, and send your healing power and may miracles and wonders be done by the name of your holy servant Jesus.

"After this prayer, the building where they were meeting shook and they were all filled with the Holy Spirit and boldly preached God's message.

"All the believers were of one heart and mind. . . ."
                                        (Acts 4:29-32)

Can you imagine sitting in a building where *all* the believers were of one heart and mind? Can you imagine the power of God that would be generated in a situation like this? No wonder the building shook! How I'd love to be sitting in a building that shook! Hallelujah!

"But Peter and the apostles replied, 'We must obey God rather than men.' "   *(Acts 5:29)*

In my searching for a total commitment to God, this verse of Scripture really came alive to me. Our obedience must always be first to God!

TIMOTHY

I Timothy 1:15-17

"How true it is, and how I long that everyone should know it, that Christ Jesus came into the world to save sinners—and I was the greatest of them all. But God had mercy on me so that Christ Jesus could use me as an example to show everyone how patient he is with even the worst sinners, so that others will realize that they, too, can have everlasting life. Glory and honor to God forever and ever. He is the King of the ages, the unseen one who never dies; he alone is God, and full of wisdom. Amen."

As I read this verse, there is such a crying out in my soul for everyone to know the truth concerning Jesus Christ. He wasn't a man who came to make our lives miserable, He came into the world to save sinners. He came to save us from sin and unhappiness and from being miserable. I've often said, "Lord, why didn't someone love me enough the first forty-nine years of my life to tell me that Jesus came to save me, and that You loved me all that time?" My heart longs to

be able to share this message with more and more people, because how my very soul rejoices when I read the
next part of that first verse. *"And I was the greatest of them
all.* But God had mercy on me so that Christ Jesus could use
me as an example to show everyone how patient He is with
even the worst sinners, so that others will realize that they,
too, can have everlasting life."

I will never be able to thank God enough or praise Him
enough for the fact that He had so much mercy on me and
how much patience He had with me. I'm sure His heart must
have cried out during those years when I was going to do it
"my" way. I'm sure He must have looked down on me and
wanted to shake me or take me to a "spiritual woodshed"
and paddle me, but He just kept on being patient with me
until I finally realized that I could have everlasting life.
God's patience is beyond Human understanding—because
His kingdom just sits there waiting year after year for
those who are willing to surrender. But why don't we do it
sooner?

All I can say is, "Glory and honor to God forever and
ever. He is the King of the ages, the unseen one who never
dies; he alone is God, and full of wisdom."

Thank You, Father. We give You the glory and honor
and praise. We thank You for the patience and love You had
for me all those years. How could I ever repay You?

I Timothy 6:1-2

"Christian slaves should work hard for their
owners and respect them; never let it be said that
Christ's people are poor workers. Don't let the
name of God or his teaching be laughed at because
of this. If their owner is a Christian, that is no
excuse for slowing down; rather they should work
all the harder because a brother in the faith is being
helped by their efforts.

>"Teach these truths, Timothy, and encourage
>all to obey them."

This is a message we proclaim as we travel around the country. Many times people feel they have been led into a ministry of one sort or another which prevents them from doing a good job for their boss. If a boss is a Christian, often they will take advantage of him. We encourage everyone to do the very best job they can, because many times the only Christian witness you will be able to give a sinner is to show him that a Christian works much harder than anyone else does. Christians should not do anything in a slothful manner, because this is a personal reflection on Jesus Christ Himself.

Look at what God's Word says: "Don't let the name of God or his teaching be laughed at because of this." Do you realize how people can laugh at Christianity just because of the way you work? And hallelujah! it can work just the reverse, too. They can see how a Christian really produces just because he is a Christian! Personalized: "Teach these truths, Frances, and encourage all to obey them."

I Timothy 6:11-12

>"Oh, Timothy, you are God's man. Run from
>all these evil things and work instead at what is
>right and good, learning to trust him and love
>others, and to be patient and gentle. Fight on for
>God. Hold tightly to the eternal life which God has
>given you, and which you have confessed with such
>a ringing confession before many witnesses."

This is one of the greatest verses in the Bible when you make it personal, as I have done here. "Oh, Frances, you are God's woman." This was one of the first ones God told me to make personal, and it took on such a completely different meaning. Many times the way to live a Christian life is explained through verses originally directed to someone else, but when made personal like this, apply to your own life. This is previously mentioned in the beginning of this book, but I wanted to include it here so it would be brought to your attention again.

I Timothy 1:21

> "Oh, Timothy, don't fail to do these things that God entrusted to you. Keep out of foolish arguments with those who boast of their 'knowledge' and thus prove their lack of it. Some of these people have missed the most important thing in life—they don't know God. May God's mercy be upon you."

One of the things that all Christians should learn is not to argue. So this is an outstanding verse to make personal. "Keep out of foolish arguments with those who boast of their 'knowledge' and thus prove their lack of it. Some of these people have missed the most important thing in life—they *don't know God!*"

I have seen Christians argue by the hour, and accomplish absolutely nothing as they get hung up on some little doctrinal point. Most of the time, people who want to argue have forgotten about God's love, and would rather spend time arguing (which is not a Christian attribute) than sharing what God is doing today . . . right NOW!

Let's not fail "to do these things that God entrusted to" us and leave the arguing to our heathen brethren. This is the time for all Christians to unite, regardless of their doctrinal differences.

Hallelujah! God is bringing together under His banner of love all denominations! Aren't you glad we're all part of the Royal Family of God?

II Timothy 1:6-8

"This being so, I want to remind you to stir into flame the strength and boldness that is in you, that entered into you when I laid my hands upon your head and blessed you. For the Holy Spirit, God's gift, does not want you to be afraid of people, but to be wise and strong, and to love them and enjoy being with them. If you will stir up this inner power, you will never be afraid to tell others about our Lord."

Did you ever look at a big pot of vegetable soup that was just sitting on a stove, not cooking, but just sitting? Would you ever guess what was underneath it? Nope, you never could until you took a spoon and stirred it and then you'd find a wealth of goodies underneath the surface. If all you did was look at the top you wouldn't find too much to get excited about. The soup has to be stirred to get all the goodness out of it, and the same thing is true of our Christian life. We have to "stir into flame the strength and boldness that is in" us. How true that God's Holy Spirit doesn't want us to be afraid of people, but to be wise and strong in the Lord. If we take a big old ladle or soup spoon and stir up the goodies that God has placed within us, we'll never be afraid to tell others about our Lord.

Hallelujah! . . . run for that ladle right now and get busy stirring, and see how many goodies you'll find underneath! There'll be an inner power there you never dreamed of which you'll never find until you start stirring.

PHILIPPIANS

Philippians 1:6

"And I am sure that God who began the good work within you will keep right on helping you grow in his grace until his task within you is finally finished on that day when Jesus Christ returns."

What a beautiful promise of God!

He will keep right on helping us until His task within us is finally finished—*on that day when Jesus Christ returns.* Isn't it wonderful to know He's not going to let us go out and flounder in the world again, but He will keep on helping us until Jesus comes, and then we won't need it anymore, because we will be in heaven with Him.

Hallelujah, Amen, Amen, and Amen!

PERSONALIZED: "And I am sure that God who began the good work within Frances will keep right on helping Frances grow in his grace until his task within Frances is finally finished on that day when Jesus Christ returns."

Philippians 1:9

> "My prayer for you is that you will overflow
> more and more with love for others, and at the
> same time keep on growing in spiritual knowledge
> and insight."

Paul and Timothy weren't just praying for the pastors
and deacons back in their days. Their same prayer is just as
effective today as God's Word says the same prayer that
"Frances will overflow more and more with love for others,
and at the same time Frances will keep on growing in
spiritual knowledge and insight."

Christianity is not just a question of getting "saved" and
then sitting down on the "saved" side of the fence and seeing
how close we can keep there so we can continue to "nibble"
in sin. *Nope*, it's a constant growing process in spiritual
knowledge and insight with a desire to overflow more and
more with love for others.

Isn't God beautiful the way He so plainly puts down in
His Word what we can expect out of the Christian life. We
can know that He's giving us the Holy Spirit power to
continue growing and being formed in His image.

Philippians 2:5-13

> "Your attitude should be the kind that was
> shown us by Jesus Christ, who, though he was
> God, did not demand and cling to his rights as
> God, but laid aside his mighty power and glory,
> taking the disguise of a slave and becoming like
> men. And he humbled himself even further, going
> so far as actually to die a criminal's death on a
> cross.
>
> "Yet it was because of this that God raised
> him up to the heights of heaven and gave him a

name which is above every other name, that at the name of Jesus every knee shall bow in heaven and on earth and under the earth, and every tongue shall confess that Jesus Christ is Lord, to the glory of God the Father.

"Dearest friends, when I was there with you, you were always so careful to follow my instructions. And now that I am away you must be even more careful to do the good things that result from being saved, obeying God with deep reverence, shrinking back from all that might displease him. For God is at work within you, helping you want to obey him, and then helping you do what he wants."

Two portions of this Scripture really stand out to me. The first one concerns the Scripture we hear quoted all the time "that at the name of Jesus every knee shall bow in heaven and on earth and under the earth, and every tongue shall confess that Jesus Christ is Lord, to the glory of God the Father." I am reminded of the number of people who feel they don't need God because of their own capabilities. I am reminded of those so involved in sin they don't even have time to think about God, and care less about Him because they don't believe He exists. How great to know that we serve a God who is all powerful and who wins the final battle, because the Bible promises that every knee shall bow—not just some, but *every* knee shall bow, and *every* tongue shall confess that Jesus Christ is Lord. It doesn't say that just some tongues are going to confess it . . . EVERY tongue in the world and even those under the earth shall confess that Jesus Christ is Lord.

I particularly love the thirteenth verse: "For God is at work within you, helping you *want* to *obey* him, and then helping you do what he wants." How fantastic to know that God is constantly working within us, helping us *want* to *obey*

Him. We can never obey God without the "want" to do so. And when you think that He is always working within us to make us have this "want," my heart just cries out in love for him. And then to think that He will then help us to do what He wants. Put your own name in this verse and see how it thrills you, or gives you a greater desire than you've ever had before. "For God is at work within Frances (hallelujah!), helping Frances WANT to OBEY him (Thank You, Jesus), and then helping Frances do what he wants."

(Thank You, God, I praise You, I worship You, I adore You for even *helping* me to do what You want me to do.) Glory!

Philippians 3:7-14

"But all these things that I once thought very worthwhile—now I've thrown them all away so that I can put my trust and hope in Christ alone. Yes, everything else is worthless when compared with the priceless gain of knowing Christ Jesus my Lord. I have put aside all else, counting it worth less than nothing, in order that I can have Christ, and become one with him, no longer counting on being saved by being good enough or by obeying God's laws, but by trusting Christ to save me; for God's way of making us right with himself depends on faith—counting on Christ alone. Now I have given up everything else—I have found it to be the only way to really know Christ and to experience the mighty power that brought him back to life again, and to find out what it means to suffer and to die with him. So, whatever it takes, I will be one who lives in the fresh newness of life of those who are alive from the dead.

"I don't mean to say I am perfect. I haven't learned all I should even yet, but I keep working toward that day when I will finally be all that Christ saved me for and wants me to be.

"No, dear brothers, I am still not all I should be but I am bringing all my energies to bear on this one thing: Forgetting the past and looking forward to what lies ahead, I strain to reach the end of the race and receive the prize for which God is calling us up to heaven because of what Christ Jesus did for us."

There are several things that really "grab" me in this portion of Scripture. First, I thank God that there was someone back in those old days who feels just like I do. Isn't it great that God hasn't changed, so we can still do the same things? We can throw away all the things we once thought were worthwhile so that we can put our trust and hope in Christ alone! People haven't changed—the things of the world may have changed somewhat, but we can still put our trust and hope in Christ alone! Paul knew this was the only way to the victorious life, and it still holds true for today.

Think of this . . . "everything else is worthless when compared with the priceless gain of knowing Christ Jesus my Lord." God's Word says it, and if it says it, it must be true . . . EVERYTHING else is worthless in comparison.

Look what Paul said: "Now I have given up everything else—I have found it to be the only way to really know Christ and to experience the mighty power that brought him back to life again." The same thing is true today if you'll put your name in there like I'm putting mine. "Now I, Frances, have given up everything else—I have found it to be the only way to really know Christ and to experience the mighty power that brought him back to life again."

This might not sound like a promise to you, but it is. If you are willing to give up everything else, and there is no question in my mind that the abundant life Jesus always talked about comes only when we are willing to give up everything else, to follow Him. As Paul says, and I agree with him wholeheartedly, "I have found it to be the only way to really know Christ and to experience the mighty power that brought him back to life again." God promises to give you the same mighty power providing you're willing to give Him ALL of you.

Thank You, Lord, for giving so much in return when we give such a very little bit—ourselves!

Doesn't it give you hope to know that Paul said, "I don't mean to say I am perfect. (Praise God, I sure haven't made it to perfection yet, have you?) I haven't learned all I should even yet (neither have I, but I'm trying), but I keep working toward that day when I will finally be all that Christ saved me for and wants me to be." (How out-of-sight to know that SOMEDAY we will be.)

PERSONALIZED: "No, dear brothers, Frances is still not all she should be but she is bringing all her energies to bear on this one thing: Forgetting the past (best advice in the world) and looking forward to what lies ahead, Frances strains to reach the end of the race and receive the prize for which God is calling Frances up to heaven because of what Christ Jesus did for her."

Well, thank You, Jesus, for holding out that big prize at the end. Thank You that even though I'm not perfect, You're letting me bring all my energies for this one thing! I love You for it!

Philippians 3:21

"When he comes back he will take these dying bodies of ours and change them into glorious bodies like his own, using the same mighty power that he will use to conquer all else everywhere."

Praise God! He's going to take this worn-out old body of mine and change it into a glorious body like His own. Just think ... no more weight problems, no more leg problems, no more aching feet after standing on them for hours—I'm going to have a brand-new body as glorious as the body of Jesus!

Lord, sometimes I think Your promises are more than I can stand.

Philippians 4:4, 6-8

"Always be full of joy in the Lord; I say it again, rejoice.

"Don't worry about anything; instead, pray about everything; tell God your needs and don't forget to thank him for his answers. If you do this you will experience God's peace, which is far more wonderful than the human mind can understand. His peace will keep your thoughts and your hearts quiet and at rest as you trust in Christ Jesus.

"And now, brothers, as I close this letter let me say this one more thing: Fix your thoughts on what is true and good and right. Think about things that are pure and lovely, and dwell on the fine, good things in others. Think about all you can praise God for and be glad about."

Christians, let your lights shine! God's Word says to ALWAYS, ALWAYS, ALWAYS be full of joy in the Lord. He even repeats it for emphasis, "I say it again, rejoice!"

Don't let the cares of the world get you down—it gives you the way out of this in the next two verses listed. The Bible just plain says: "Don't worry about ANYTHING; instead, pray about everything; tell God your needs and don't forget to thank him for his answers."

If we could just understand that God doesn't want us to worry—Jesus is the answer—what's your problem? See what I mean? You've got the answer before the problem ever comes up. Instead, God tells you to pray about everything (no exceptions either), but then watch that next little condition. "Don't forget to thank him for his answers." So many times we have seen people receive miracles, who forget to stop and thank Him. Be sure you always take time out to thank Him for His answers (even though the answer might not be exactly the way you thought it was going to be).

Look at what He promises if you do what He tells you to. "You will experience God's peace, which is far more wonderful than the human mind can understand. His peace will keep your thoughts and your hearts quiet and at rest as you trust in Christ Jesus."

Meditate and concentrate on what that says! What could be more wonderful to have than God's peace in a world of turmoil, frustration and tension? And yet it's there because God's Word promises it. I like to put my own name right in front of that promise: "Frances, if you do this you will experience God's peace, which is far more wonderful than the human mind can understand." Hallelujah! God's Word has said it and God's Word cannot lie, so the peace of God is mine.

"Frances, think about things that are pure and lovely, and dwell on the fine, good things in others." Aren't we all better off when we do this? Put your own name in there right now.

"Frances, think about ALL you can PRAISE God for and be glad about." Spend your time thinking about what you can praise God for, instead of the things you might be tempted to complain about.

Do you realize how much God must have loved us to have inspired these men of old to put down on paper the simple things that make the Christian life so exciting!

Philippians 4:13

"For I can do everything God asks me to with the help of Christ who gives me the strength and power."

What a well-known verse, but what a beautiful verse to remember that you can do EVERYTHING God asks you to. This is another real good one to put your name in. And just think as you do, what a promise this is:

"For Frances can do everything God asks her to with the help of Christ who gives Frances the strength and power."

There have been many times when I felt I was so tired I couldn't possibly continue any longer. There have been many times when our schedule has been so grueling I felt in the natural there wasn't any way I could stay on my feet for another service, and yet the minute we stand up in front of a congregation, the anointing of God falls, and there is no doubt whatsoever that we can do "everything God asks us to . . ." Why? Because of the help of Christ who gives us the strength and power. God never asks you to do more than He will give you the strength and power to do.

Praise You, Jesus! We thank You for these wonderful promises scattered all throughout Your Word.

CORINTHIANS

I Corinthians 1:7

"Now you have every grace and blessing; every spiritual gift and power for doing his will are yours during this time of waiting for the return of our Lord Jesus Christ."

Do you hear that beautiful promise of God? "Now you have every grace and blessing; *every spiritual gift and power* for doing his will are yours during this time of waiting for the return of our Lord Jesus Christ."

Can you imagine that you possess every single grace and blessing (if you claim them) and even more than that, EVERY spiritual gift and power for doing His will. Did you ever really stop to think what a promise this is? Not just a little power is promised, but every spiritual gift and power are yours.

God never asks us to do anything that He hasn't already made a provision for the gifts to do them and the power to accomplish what He has called us for. And yet none of it is our own—it is all His Power which He so freely gives to us. Thank You, Jesus!

PERSONALIZED: "Frances, now you have every grace and blessing; every spiritual gift and power for doing his will are yours during this time of waiting for the return of our Lord Jesus Christ!"

I Corinthians 1:21

> "For God in his wisdom saw to it that the world would never find God through human brilliance, and then he stepped in and saved all those who believed his message, which the world calls foolish and silly."

Just think, God didn't devise a plan where we had to be brilliant; He said all we had to do was just believe. What a beautiful promise that our salvation depends not on our own human intellect, but on our believing!

I Corinthians 10:13

> "But remember this—the wrong desires that come into your life aren't anything new and different. Many others have faced exactly the same problems before you. And no temptation is irresistible. You can trust God to keep the temptation from becoming so strong that you can't stand up against it, for he has promised this and will do what he says. He will show you how to escape temptation's power so that you can bear up patiently against it."

Do you really believe that your temptations and problems are different from anyone else's? They're not! It says so right in God's Holy Word. Isn't it a beautiful promise to know that many others have faced exactly the same problems you are facing right now? So relax!

Regardless of what your temptation is, if you stand upon His promises you can know that "He will show you how to escape temptation's power."

PERSONALIZED: "But remember this—the wrong desires that come into Frances' life aren't anything new and different. Many others have faced exactly the same problems before Frances. And no temptation is irresistible. Frances can trust God to keep the temptation from becoming so strong that Frances can't stand up against it, for he has promised this and will do what he says. He will show Frances how to escape temptation's power so that Frances can bear up patiently against it."

Thank You, dear Jesus!

II Corinthians 5:17

"When someone becomes a Christian he becomes a brand-new person inside. He is not the same any more. A new life has begun!"

This is one of the few verses where I like the *King James* version better: "Therefore if any man be in Christ, he is a new creature: old things are passed away; behold, all things are become new."

And this is exactly the way it has to be. If we are really in Christ, God's Word says that we are a brand-new person—a brand-new creature. The old one who had a temper is gone . . . the old one who had a nasty disposition is gone . . . the old one who had a critical spirit is gone. . . . We are brand-new creatures, "Therefore . . . the old things are passed away; behold, ALL things are become new."

This isn't just a casual statement—this is a true and correct statement. All things are become new. Instead of irritation and frustration, there will be peace. Instead of hate, there will be love. Instead of misery, there will be joy. Instead of impatience, there will be patience and understanding. Instead of being unkind, there will be kindness. Instead of riding roughshod over everyone, there will be gentleness. These are all promises of God! Let's turn in all the attitudes that belonged to the old creature and take up the new ones of the new creature. They're ours because of God's promises.

Bless the Lord, oh, my soul, and all that is within me, bless His Holy Name!

PERSONALIZED: "When Frances became a Christian she became a brand-new person inside. Frances is not the same any more. A new life has begun!"

Hallelujah!

II Corinthians 5:18-21

"All these new things are from God who brought us back to himself through what Christ Jesus did. And God has given us the privilege of urging everyone to come into his favor and be reconciled to him. For God was in Christ, restoring the world to himself, no longer counting men's sins against them but blotting them out. This is the wonderful message he has given us to tell others. We are Christ's ambassadors. God is using us to speak to you: we beg you, as though Christ himself were here pleading with you, receive the love he offers you—be reconciled to God. For God took the sinless Christ and poured into him our sins. Then, in exchange, he poured God's goodness into us."

I'm only going to share a couple of things in this verse. "For God was in Christ, restoring the world to himself, *no longer counting men's sins against them* but blotting them out. This is the wonderful message he has given us to tell others."

What a promise of God that He no longer counts your sins, but has blotted them out. Hallelujah! And then listen to the next! I think of how many times I have tried to sell people on "ideas" in the printing business. We always had to think of ideas to help stores sell merchandise, and yet today I think of the job God has given me—to simply tell others that He has blotted out their sins. Glory . . . !

Listen to what it says next: (making it personal) "Charles and Frances are Christ's ambassadors. God is using Charles and Frances to speak to you: we beg you, as though Christ himself were here pleading with you, receive the love he offers you—be reconciled to God."

What a promise of God that we are His ambassadors! Glory, who has a better employer than we do?

Now listen to the final promise in this portion of Scripture as it is made personal in my own life:

"For God took the sinless Christ and poured into him Frances Hunter's sins. Then in exchange, he poured God's goodness into Frances!"

The first time I was ever really aware of what God had done for me was through this particular little verse. Just picture in your mind if you can, two vials (test tubes) like in a chemistry lab. One vial is Jesus—the other one is you. One vial is sinless—the other one has all of your sins. God took the sinless vial which is Christ, and just dumped all of your nasty sins right into that vial. That's what Jesus got from you.

Now . . . what did you get from Him? The promise of God says: "Then in exchange, he poured God's goodness into us!"

Oh, come let us adore Him. How could we help but worship and adore Him when He makes exchanges like this? Lift your hands right now and let's just take time out to worship Him, shall we?

MATTHEW

Matthew 6:33

"But seek first his kingdom and his righteousness, and all these things shall be yours as well."
(From the *Revised Standard*)

This was the verse that was so meaningful when I was
searching God's Word for the answer as to whether or not I
was to marry Charles. When I saw it, I realized that
everything in life falls in place AFTER you seek first the
kingdom of God and His righteousness. If we could just
remember to always be seeking God, we'd never have to
worry about anything else, because everything would be
added to us if we only did that one thing!

Matthew 7:13-14

I am quoting this Scripture from the *Revised Standard
Bible*, because it appeals to me more in this version than any
other. It could be because I was reading the *Revised Standard*
as a new Christian, and God spoke so plainly to me to
remember that the gate to heaven is a very narrow one.

"Enter by the narrow gate; for the gate is wide and the way is easy, that leads to destruction, and those who enter by it are many. For the gate is narrow and the way is hard, that leads to life, and those who find it are few."

Let's keep our eyes heavenward, remembering that the road is narrow that leads to eternal life, and if we turn our eyes to things away from heaven, we can be distracted and end up on the wide road.

The Living Bible is just as emphatic:

"Heaven can be entered only through the narrow gate! The highway to hell is broad, and its gate is wide enough for all the multitudes who choose its easy way. But the Gateway to Life is small, and the road is narrow, and only a few ever find it!"

I JOHN

I John 1:5-7

"This is the message God has given us to pass
on to you: that God is Light and in him is no
darkness at all. So if we say we are his friends, but
go on living in spiritual darkness and sin, we are
lying. But if we are living in the light of God's
presence, just as Christ does, then we have wonderful fellowship and joy with each other, and the
blood of Jesus his Son cleanses us from every sin."

How magnificent to know that God is Light and in Him
is no darkness at all. Nothing, nothing, nothing of darkness is
in Him, and there's no point in trying to deceive Him, because He says if we go on living in spiritual darkness and
sin, we are lying. But Hallelujah! we can live in the light
of God's presence, just as Christ does. Just another one of
those beautiful reminders to lead a holy life.

Let's see what this sounds like on a personal basis: "This
is the message God has given us to pass on to Frances: that
God is Light and in him is no darkness at all. So if Frances

says she is his friend, but goes on living in spiritual darkness and sin, she is lying. But if Frances is living in the light of God's presence, just as Christ does, then we have wonderful fellowship and joy with each other, and the blood of Jesus his Son cleanses Frances from every sin."

Glory to God for His wonderful promises!

I John 1:9

> "If we confess our sins, he is faithful and just, and will forgive our sins and cleanse us from all unrighteousness."

I just had to quote this verse from the *Revised Standard,* because it seems just a little bit plainer than the other translations. So many times after people become Christians, they don't know what to do when a sin creeps into their life, or for a moment they say or do something that isn't becoming to a Christian. Do we just ignore it and go on our way, walking with God? Do we wait until Sunday and then confess it to the pastor or priest?

No, God's Word says if we'll confess, He'll forgive, and the time to do it is right NOW! Guilt can take the joy out of your Christian life, and to go around with guilt on your shoulders is so unnecessary for a Christian. Confess whatever happens the moment it happens, and your fellowship with God is restored, and then go on walking in the light!

Every once in a while, I might forget the speed limit and go five or so miles over it, but the minute I am aware of it, I say, "Lord, forgive me!" And His forgiveness is there, and I can go on walking moment by moment under the control of the Holy Spirit, within the speed limit!

You can always be assured that God will do His part, when you do YOUR part!

Hallelujah!

JUDE

Jude 1:24-25

"And now—all glory to him who alone is God, who saves us through Jesus Christ our Lord; yes, splendor and majesty, all power and authority are his from the beginning; his they are and his they evermore shall be. And he is able to keep you from slipping and falling away, and to bring you, sinless and perfect, into his glorious presence with mighty shouts of everlasting joy."

Read that out loud, will you, and see how it affects you. It just thrills my soul to read about the splendor, majesty, power and authority which belong to Him. And because of this, He is able to keep Frances from slipping and falling away so as to bring Frances SINLESS and PERFECT, into His glorious presence with mighty shouts of everlasting joy!

No amount of effort on our part could ever make us sinless and perfect, but because of a promise of God we can rest assured that that's exactly the way we'll be brought into His glorious presence. Glory!

LUKE

Luke 1:26-38

Every chapter has something real special, and I love the entire book of Luke. However, these are my "very" favorites.

"The following month God sent the angel Gabriel to Nazareth, a village in Galilee to a virgin, Mary, engaged to be married to a man named Joseph, a descendant of King David.

"Gabriel appeared to her and said, 'Congratulations, favored lady! The Lord is with you.'

"Confused and disturbed, Mary tried to think what the angel could mean.

" 'Don't be frightened, Mary,' the angel told her, 'for God has decided to wonderfully bless you! Very soon now, you will become pregnant and have a baby boy, and you are to name him 'Jesus.' He shall be very great and shall be called the Son of God. And the Lord God shall give him the throne of his ancestor David. And he shall reign over Israel forever; his Kingdom shall never end!'

"Mary asked the angel. 'But how can I have a baby? I am a virgin.'

"The angel replied, 'The Holy Spirit shall come upon you, and the power of God shall overshadow you; so the baby born to you will be utterly holy—the Son of God. Furthermore, six months ago your Aunt Elizabeth—'the barren one,' they called her—became pregnant in her old age: For every promise from God shall surely come true.'

"Mary said, 'I am the Lord's servant, and I am willing to do whatever he wants. May everything you said come true.' And then the angel disappeared."

Whether it's Christmastime or any other time during the year, I love this part of Luke because of one little sentence almost at the end of it. I have tried to envision myself as Mary—I have tried to envision my daughter as Mary, to see if it would be possible to have the kind of feelings and questions she must have had at that moment when the angel Gabriel appeared to her. What would she tell her Mother? How could she explain her pregnancy to her betrothed, Joseph? How could she explain it to her friends? What would happen to her own life. I tried to visualize Joan coming home and telling me some story like this—how would I have reacted? Mary was a very young girl and there must have been a myriad of thoughts run through her mind at this moment, and while the Bible doesn't record how long it took for her to make a decision—it seems a very short time!

Mary's answer is one of the most beautiful answers of anyone in the entire Bible because of its simplicity: "I am the Lord's servant, and *I am willing to do whatever he wants.*"

Regardless of cost, regardless of consequences, regardless of the favor of her fiance or family, Mary said without hesitation, "I am willing to do whatever He wants."

God challenges me every time I read this! "Are YOU willing to do whatever I want?"

Yes, Lord!

Luke 3:16-17

> "John answered the question by saying, 'I
> baptize only with water; but someone is coming
> soon who has far higher authority than mine; in
> fact, I am not even worthy of being his slave. He
> will baptize you with fire—with the Holy Spirit. He
> will separate chaff from grain, and burn up the
> chaff with eternal fire and store away the grain.' "

I especially love this Scripture because of the great
promise it contains: "He will baptize Frances with FIRE—
with the Holy Spirit." I had read so many times the glorious
account of the day of Pentecost and how the fire came down
on their heads and how I believed that even in this day and
time Jesus would still baptize with FIRE! What a promise to
every born-again believer. We don't have to wonder and
guess, we can KNOW from His Word that He will baptize us
with Fire! Hallelujah!

Luke 4:18-19

> "The Spirit of the Lord is upon me; he has
> appointed me to preach Good News to the poor;
> he has sent me to heal the brokenhearted and to
> announce that captives shall be released and the
> blind shall see, that the downtrodden shall be freed
> from their oppressors, and that God is ready to
> give blessings to all who come to him."

From the moment I was saved, there has been an
overwhelming urge and desire in my life to share the Good
News with everyone I come in contact with. *I find it impossible to talk about the things of the world, when the only
thing that ever seems worthwhile to me is Jesus and His love!*

This verse sums it all up so beautifully!

Luke 4:40

> "As the sun went down that evening, all the
> villagers who had any sick people in their homes,
> no matter what their diseases were, brought them
> to Jesus; and the touch of his hands healed every
> one!"

From the moment of my conversion, I have been
absolutely fascinated by Jesus' healing power. Somehow this
verse has always been extra special because of the last little
phrase: "And the touch of his hands healed every one!" Isn't
that beautiful, and can't you just feel the touch of Jesus'
hands on you right now, healing your every need and
problem?

Luke 6:38

> "For if you give, you will get! Your gift will
> return to you in full and overflowing measure,
> pressed down, shaken together to make room for
> more, and running over. Whatever measure you use
> to give—large or small—will be used to measure
> what is given back to you."

I guess the first place God got me was in the
pocketbook because He told me the devil had had my money
long enough, and now He wanted it. I didn't understand the
principles of God at all, but I gave because I WANTED TO! I
had so fallen in love with God that I didn't want anything for
myself—I only wanted everything for Him! And so I gave and
gave and gave and unknowingly tapped into one of the
greatest truths in the Bible! God gave back to me so
generously, I had to turn around and give back to Him. And
then He gave back to me (in accordance with His Word) and
we've had a running battle all the years I've been a Christian,

and I've never been able to outgive Him. But who could? No one, if you listened to what God's Word says. And it's beautiful that He returns to us with the same measure we give to Him. If we're generous, then He, by His Word, has to be generous with us. Glory!

This applies not only to money, but to your own self. If you give yourself to God, then He, by His Word, has to give back to you, but what an exchange He makes. He gives you Himself through the person of His Son Jesus, in exchange for you. (I certainly got the best end of that trade; how about you?)

Let's make the verse personal now, and see how it sounds: "For if Frances gives, she will get! Frances' gift will return to her in full and overflowing measure, pressed down, shaken together to make room for more, and running over. Whatever measure Frances uses to give—large or small—will be used to measure what is given back to Frances."

Let's really think about that verse very carefully because it can alter the course of your entire Christian life. Did you know that you choose the measure that God is going to use to bless you? He doesn't choose it—you choose it, and it's the measure that you use to give to Him that He (by His Word) has to use in returning to you. Thank You, Jesus!

Recently we were in Jacksonville Beach, Florida and our motel was right on the ocean. On Sunday morning we were looking out the window prior to going to church and I saw a perfect example of the way God returns to us.

There was a little child, probably no more than one-and-a-half or two-years-old, sitting on the beach with a tiny little scoop, shoveling away, trying to fill up a little bucket. He was working so hard, and it was taking so many scoops to fill his little bucket because his scoop was a real tiny little one.

Just a little farther down the beach sat a big crane, waiting for Monday to come and the operator to begin taking big bites out of the earth for some construction work. I looked at the little scoop of the baby, and then looked at the huge scoop on the crane, and it was so simple to understand this Scripture now! The little scoop was only capable of picking up so much, and no more because its size was limited! The big crane literally bit huge chunks out of the earth, in the same amount of time.

God (by His Word) has to return to us by the measure we use to give to Him—if it's a little child's scoop, then He has to use the same thing. If we give to Him with the scoop of a big crane, then His Word says He will use the same big scoop to return to us.

Hallelujah! Give me a big scoop!

Luke 7:36-50

"One of the Pharisees asked Jesus to come to his home for lunch and Jesus accepted the invitation. As they sat down to eat, a woman of the streets—a prostitute—heard he was there and brought an exquisite flask filled with expensive perfume. Going in, she knelt behind him at his feet, weeping, with her tears falling down upon his feet; and she wiped them off with her hair and kissed them and poured the perfume on them.

"When Jesus' host, a Pharisee, saw what was happening and who the woman was, he said to himself, 'This proves that Jesus is no prophet, for if God had really sent him, he would know what kind of woman this one is!'

"Then Jesus spoke up and answered his thoughts. 'Simon,' he said to the Pharisee, 'I have something to say to you.'

" 'All right, Teacher,' Simon replied, 'go ahead.'

"Then Jesus told him this story: 'A man loaned money to two people—$5,000 to one and

$500 to the other. But neither of them could pay him back, so he kindly forgave them both, letting them keep the money! Which do you suppose loved him most after that?'

" 'I suppose the one who had owed him the most,' Simon answered.

" 'Correct,' Jesus agreed.

"Then he turned to the woman and said to Simon, 'Look! See this woman kneeling here! When I entered your home, you didn't bother to offer me water to wash the dust from my feet, but she has washed them with her tears and wiped them with her hair. You refused me the customary kiss of greeting, but she has kissed my feet again and again from the time I first came in. You neglected the usual courtesy of olive oil to anoint my head, but she has covered my feet with rare perfume. Therefore her sins—and they are many—are forgiven, for she loved me much; but one who is forgiven little, shows little love.'

"And he said to her, 'Your sins are forgiven.'

"Then the men at the table said to themselves, 'Who does this man think he is, going around forgiving sins?'

"And Jesus said to the woman, 'Your faith has saved you; go in peace.' "

This really speaks to me because of the woman's willingness to give her all—her love, her affection, her worldly possessions and probably the thing that was the most dear to her, but she willingly poured it on Jesus' feet. God dealt with me so many times concerning total and complete commitment that this verse really spoke of being willing to give "all" to Jesus. At the top of my Bible on this page I have written "Some people only want to be forgiven little because they aren't willing to give ALL!"

Luke 9:23-25

"Then he said to all, 'Anyone who wants to follow me must put aside his own desires and conveniences and carry his cross with him every day and *keep close to me!* Whoever loses his life for my sake will save it, but whoever insists on keeping his life will lose it; and what profit is there in gaining the whole world when it means forfeiting one's self?' "

I like this because it constantly reminds me to keep close to Jesus, and never stray away! The middle sentence says so much about giving everything to Jesus and giving up "self" because when we insist on keeping "self" we run into problems; but when we're willing to lose our life in the shadow of Jesus, we will gain eternal life, and who could ask for anything more. The last sentence shows how useless it is to try to gain the whole world when you end up losing your own soul.

Don't look at this as a condemning Scripture, but look at it for the promises it contains.

Look at the glory when you make the verse personal: "If Frances wants to follow me she must put aside her own desires and conveniences and carry her cross with her every day and keep close to me! If Frances loses her life for my sake she will save it, but if she insists on keeping her life will lose it; and what profit is there in Frances gaining the whole world when it means forfeiting herself?" None, Lord Jesus, absolutely none. Thank You for making the choice so easy!

Luke 10:19-21

"And I have given you authority over all the power of the Enemy, and to walk among serpents and scorpions and to crush them. Nothing shall injure you! However, the important thing is not that demons obey you, but that your names are registered as citizens of heaven.

"Then he was filled with the joy of the Holy Spirit and said, 'I praise you, O Father, Lord of heaven and earth, for hiding these things from the intellectuals and worldly wise and for revealing them to those who are as trusting as little children.' "

Beautiful, beautiful, beautiful, when we realize that Jesus has given us authority over ALL the power of the Enemy. There is nothing that Satan can do to you, because you have the authority over ALL, every single bit, of the power of the Enemy. God's Word says that *nothing shall injure you!* And yet He makes it so plain that your power is really unimportant alongside the most important thing of all, and that is that your name is written in the Book of Life. Hallelujah!

Praise God He makes these simple little truths so easy to find, that even a little child can find them because of their simple trust.

Try it on a personal basis: "And I have given Frances authority over all the power of the Enemy, and to walk among serpents and scorpions and to crush them. Nothing shall injure Frances! However, the important thing is not that demons obey Frances, but that Frances' name is registered as a citizen of heaven."

Thank You, Jesus, for writing my name in that book!

Luke 11:33-36

"No one lights a lamp and hides it! Instead, he puts it on a lampstand to give light to all who enter the room. Your eyes light up your inward being. A pure eye lets sunshine into your soul. A lustful eye shuts out the light and plunges you into darkness. So watch out that the sunshine isn't blotted out. If you are filled with light within, with no dark corners, then your face will be radiant too, as though a floodlight is beamed upon you."

What a beautiful comparison—a light illumined by electricity, and a face, illuminated by the Spirit of God! I think of the radiant faces of Christians who look like they almost swallowed a light bulb.

When Charles and I get off a plane in a strange city, and don't know who is going to meet us to take us to our meetings, we always look for the ones with the radiant faces as though there was a floodlight beamed on them. . . . It never fails—we can always pick out the Christian who is going to pick us up by the inner glow which shines outside too. Glory!!!

Look what happens in the personalization of the thirty-sixth verse. "If Frances is filled with light within, with no dark corners, then Frances' face will be radiant too, as though a floodlight is beamed upon her."

Hallelujah, Jesus, turn that floodlight on!

Luke 14:26-27

"Anyone who wants to be my follower must love me far more than he does his own father, mother, wife, children, brothers, or sisters—yes, more than his own life—otherwise he cannot be my disciple. And no one can be my disciple who does not carry his own cross and follow me."

I believe with all my heart, that every committed Christian faces a decision at one time or another in their life as to whom they love the most. God has given all of us a supernatural love for our husbands and children, but when we get to that point of total commitment, we have to be willing to choose to love God more than any member of our family. The most beautiful part of all this, however, is that when you love God more than anyone in the world, He will give you a greater ability to love every member of your family than you ever dreamed of.

That's just like God, though, isn't it? When you give Him your first love, He gives back far more than you could ever hope to give Him. Not only in His love, but in your ability to love your own husband and children more than before.

The day that God confronted me with that Scripture, He said: "If Frances wants to be my follower she must love me far more than she does her own father, mother, Tom, Joan (children), brothers, or sisters—yes more than Frances' own life—otherwise she cannot be my disciple. And no one (including Frances) can be my disciple if she does not carry her own cross and follow me."

JOHN

The book of John contains many of my favorite Scriptures. This is one of the greatest books to make personal in the entire Bible because it really allows Jesus to speak to you in one of the most intimate of all books, if you will let Him. It is almost impossible to try and pick out the "favorite" verses without the entire book, so I am going to leave out some of those most commonly used, and try to show you some verses that many times are not particularly emphasized.

John 3:1-8

"After dark one night a Jewish religious leader named Nicodemus, a member of the sect of the Pharisees, came for an interview with Jesus. 'Sir,' he said, 'we all know that God has sent you to teach us. Your miracles are proof enough of this.'

"Jesus replied, 'With all the earnestness I possess I tell you this: Unless you are born again, you can never get into the Kingdom of God.'

" 'Born again!' exclaimed Nicodemus. 'What do you mean? How can an old man go back into his mother's womb and be born again?'

"Jesus replied, 'What I am telling you so earnestly is this: Unless one is born of water and the Spirit, he cannot enter the Kingdom of God. Men can only reproduce human life, but the Holy Spirit gives new life from heaven; so don't be surprised at my statement that you must be born again! Just as you can hear the wind but can't tell where it comes from or where it will go next, so it is with the Spirit. We do not know on whom he will next bestow this life from heaven.' "

To me this is one of the most beautiful Scriptures in the Bible, because it was this portion that made me realize I was not a Christian. So many times we can be involved in church work, the usual tuna fish and cream cheese sandwich type of Christianity, without knowing that we can have a personal relationship with Jesus Christ. The first time I ever heard this portion of Scripture, I completely fell apart and panicked, because I realized that even with a lifetime of spasmodic church attendance, good works, etc., that I had never been born "again" or born from above. My first panic-stricken thought was, "I CAN'T LET GOD KNOW—HE THINKS I'M A CHRISTIAN!"

How deceived we can be by Satan into honestly thinking we are Christians and yet discovering later that we are wearing a counterfeit Christian halo. I love the Bible because there is no gray in it—it is black or white. "You either 'is,' or you 'ain't.' " It's as simple as that. You have either been born again, or you haven't been born again. And isn't it exciting to know there's no "maybe" involved. The Bible is so specific in saying, "Unless one is born of water (when you're born physically), and the Spirit (when you're born again), *he cannot enter the kingdom of God.*" Nothing that you do through good works on this earth can get you into heaven; it's a question of being born again, which is so simple. It's just a question of asking God to forgive your sins and asking Jesus to come into your heart.

Maybe as you read this you are aware of the fact that you have never been born again, or maybe there's doubt. Would you like to pray a simple little prayer right now, just to make sure that you know *that you know* that you KNOW that you've been born again? This is the prayer (word for word) that I prayed when I became a Christian. "Lord Jesus, forgive my sins. I open the door of my life and receive You as my Savior and Lord. Take control of the throne of my life. Make me the kind of person You want me to be. Thank You for coming into my heart and for hearing my prayer as You promised."

May I ask you a question right now? Where is Jesus Christ? IN YOUR HEART! Hallelujah!

John 4:6-29

"He had to go through Samaria on the way, and around noon as he approached the village of Sychar, he came to Jacob's Well, located on the parcel of ground Jacob gave to his son Joseph. Jesus was tired from the long walk in the hot sun and sat wearily beside the well.

"Soon a Samaritan woman came to draw water, and Jesus asked her for a drink. He was alone at the time as his disciples had gone into the village to buy some food. The woman was surprised that a Jew would ask a 'despised Samaritan' for anything—usually they wouldn't even speak to them!—and she remarked about this to Jesus.

"He replied, 'If you only knew what a wonderful gift God has for you, and who I am, you would ask me for some *living* water.'

" 'But you don't have a rope or a bucket,' she said, 'and this is a very deep well! Where would you get this living water? And besides, are you greater than our ancestor Jacob? How can you offer better water than this which he and his sons and cattle enjoyed?'

"Jesus replied that people soon became thirsty again after drinking this water. 'But the water I give them,' he said, 'becomes a perpetual spring within them, watering them forever with eternal life.'

" 'Please, sir,' the woman said, 'give me some of that water! Then I'll never be thirsty again and won't have to make this long trip out here every day.'

" 'Go and get your husband,' Jesus told her.

" 'But I'm not married,' the woman replied.

" 'All too true!' Jesus said. 'For you have had five husbands, and you aren't even married to the man you're living with now.'

" 'Sir,' the woman said, 'you must be a prophet. But say, tell me, why is it that you Jews insist that Jerusalem is the only place of worship, while we Samaritans claim it is here [at Mount Gerazim], where our ancestors worshiped?'

"Jesus replied, 'The time is coming, ma'am, when we will no longer be concerned about whether to worship the Father here or in Jerusalem. For it's not *where* we worship that counts, but *how* we worship—is our worship spiritual and real? Do we have the Holy Spirit's help? For God is Spirit, and we must have his help to worship as we should. The Father wants this kind of worship from us. But you Samaritans know so little about him, worshiping blindly, while we Jews know all about him, for salvation comes to the world through the Jews.'

"The woman said, 'Well, at least I know that the Messiah will come—the one they call Christ—and when he does, he will explain everything to us.'

"Then Jesus told her, 'I am the Messiah!'

"Just then his disciples arrived. They were surprised to find him talking to a woman, but none of them asked him why, or what they had been discussing.

"Then the woman left her waterpot beside the well and went back to the village and told everyone, 'Come and meet a man who told me everything I ever did!' "

This is a well-known story in the Bible because it's one of the most beautiful to show the compassion of Jesus toward even the worst of sinners, and it gives one of the greatest promises of the Bible. "If you only knew what a wonderful gift God has for you, and who I am, YOU WOULD ASK ME FOR SOME LIVING WATER!" The same thing is true of each and every one of us. If we really understood who Jesus is, even the greatest unbeliever would come seeking the *living water.* And then listen to this fabulous promise in the Word of God: "The water I give them becomes a perpetual spring within them, watering them forever with eternal life." When Jesus gives you the living water, it becomes a perpetual (flowing forever and forever) stream within you, watering you FOREVER with eternal life. God has so much to say, and so much to give, if we will just believe.

Reading down just a little bit farther, is also another great truth. "For it's not WHERE we worship that counts, but HOW we worship—is our worship spiritual and real? Do we have the Holy Spirit's help? For God is Spirit, and we must have his help to worship as we should. The Father WANTS this kind of worship from us." The Father wants us to worship Him and so many times we don't take enough time to really worship Him.

Then look at what the woman at the well told everyone: "Come and meet a man who told me *everything* I ever did!" I believe the thing that really convicted me of the fact that I was a sinner—and I had an awful time ever admitting to God that I was a sinner, let alone to myself (that awful PRIDE stood in the way)—was when God whispered in my ear one Sunday morning and said "Frances, I know every rotten, stinking thing you've ever done (that didn't surprise me); I know every rotten, stinking thing you've ever said (that didn't surprise me too much); I know every rotten, stinking thing you've ever thought." That last statement, which was spoken so softly into my mind, brought my entire world crashing down when I realized that God even knew every single thought that had ever entered my mind! Without a doubt I could no longer question the fact that I was a sinner. And look at the woman at the well—the thing that convinced her was because Jesus knew all about her.

Beloved, isn't it beautiful to know that God knows all about us, but in spite of it all, is willing to forgive us and wash us white as snow! Glory!

John 6:35, 47-51

> "Jesus replied, 'I am the Bread of Life. No one coming to me will ever be hungry again. Those believing in me will never thirst.
>
> "How earnestly I tell you this—anyone who believes in me already has eternal life! Yes, I am the Bread of Life! When your fathers in the wilderness ate bread from the skies, they all died. But the Bread from heaven gives eternal life to everyone who eats it. I am that Living Bread that came down out of heaven. Anyone eating this Bread shall live forever; this Bread is my flesh given to redeem humanity."

John 7:37

> " 'If anyone is thirsty, let him come to me
> and drink. For the Scriptures declare that rivers of
> living water shall flow from the inmost being of
> anyone who believes in me.' (He was speaking of
> the Holy Spirit, who would be given to everyone
> believing in him. . . .)' '

I have grouped three Scriptures together here because
they all basically relate to the same subject, and all give the
same promise concerning the fact that those who hunger and
thirst after righteousness shall never hunger and thirst again.
No one ever eating of the Bread of Life will ever be hungry
again and those drinking the Living Water will never thirst.

This doesn't mean just a drop in the beginning, and no
more ever again, but a constant drinking of the Living Water
of Life. Anyone eating the Bread shall live forever (what a
promise!). Then listen to what it says if you do drink:
"Rivers of living water shall flow from the inmost being of
anyone who believes in me."

Just think, because of the Holy Spirit living within you,
rivers of this same water shall flow from you to quench the
thirst of others, just like it did from Jesus! Hallelujah!

John 8:12

> "Jesus said to the people, 'I am the Light of
> the world. So if you follow me, you won't be
> stumbling through the darkness, for living light will
> flood your path.' "

We used this verse of Scripture on one of our Christmas
cards one year becasue it gives such a promise to the world.
How many of us stumble around month after month in the
darkness, trying to do it "our own way" instead of letting the

living Light lead us, because if we follow after Jesus, He will flood our path with His light! Hallelujah, what a promise to know that we don't have to do it on our own because He makes it so easy for us, and always so beautiful. No more stumbling when you follow Jesus.

John 8:31-32

> "Jesus said to them, 'You are truly my disciples if you live as I tell you to, and you will know the truth, and the truth will set you free.' "

What a promise. Stated so simply and yet so beautifully and so positively. "You are truly my disciples if you live as I tell you to," and here's the promise, "and you will know the truth, and the truth will set you free." Did you see the condition preceding the promise? It was the fact that we are truly His disciples if we live as He tells us to, and then, after that we will know the truth, and the truth will set us free.

The King James translation puts it a little differently, but the meaning seems the same to me. "If ye continue in my word (or obey me, or live as I tell you to), then are ye my disciples indeed; and ye shall know the truth, and the truth shall make you free."

The beauty of knowing we can live a life completely FREE is there because of God's Word and Jesus' promise to us. He doesn't say either that it will make us partially free—He says it will make us *free* . . . all the way! Thank You, Jesus!

John 8:51

> "With all the earnestness I have I tell you this—no one who obeys me shall ever die!"

What a completely satisfying promise from Jesus. All we have to do is to obey Him, and we have His promise that we will never die. Hallelujah! What fear does death hold when we know that all it takes is obedience to have eternal life.

What else promises you this? Do any of the things of the world? Nope, only Jesus! But, praise God! the promise is there.

John 9:31

"Well, God doesn't listen to evil men, but he has open ears to those who worship him and do his will."

That little verse ought to give you great hope. How much simpler can you get? We wonder how to make God listen to us. Did you really read that? God has open ears to those who worship Him and do His will. No more, no less! He doesn't listen to people who aren't interested in doing His will, but to those who do, He has open ears.

Father, we praise You because of the simplicity of Your Word.

John 14:22-24

" 'Sir, why are you going to reveal yourself only to us disciples and not to the world at large?'

"Jesus replied, 'Because I will only reveal myself to those who love me and obey me. The Father will love them too, and we will come to them and live with them. Anyone who doesn't obey me doesn't love me. And remember, I am not making up this answer to your question! It is the answer given by the Father who sent me.' "

I just love this verse of Scripture because even though it holds a beautiful promise, it also holds some news which might not be so good to those who don't really love Jesus!

Jesus doesn't indiscriminately reveal Himself and all of His goodness to everyone, but He so beautifully states that He will do this only for those who love Him and obey Him.

And He lets you know right where He stands, too, because He says if you don't obey Him, you just plain don't love Him. It's as simple as that. When you love Him, the only desire of your heart will be to obey Him and do whatever He wants you to, and nothing else.

But how beautiful to know that His love is unending and bountiful to those who do what He says.

John 14:27

> "I am leaving you with a gift—peace of mind and heart! And the peace I give isn't fragile like the peace the world gives. So don't be troubled or afraid."

Did you hear what Jesus promised? *Peace of mind and heart!* Beloved, if we would just learn the promises of God, our lives could be without frustration and fear. Jesus said it, and I believe it. He said, "I am leaving you with a gift—peace of mind and heart!" If He didn't promise another thing, that would be enough. Believe Him, and accept His gift of peace of mind and heart! Don't let your heart be troubled, because He's right there to give you a peace that isn't fragile like the peace the world gives. His peace is indestructible once you allow Him to give it to you.

John 15:5, 7

> "For apart from me you can't do a thing. . . . But if you stay in me and obey my commands, you may ask any request you like, and it will be granted!"

I love this promise that Jesus made. He wanted to make sure that we didn't try to continue to do it on our own, but that we would rely on Him, because He so simply stated, "For apart from me you can't do a thing." You might not look on this as a promise, but I do. He just promises that you'll fail if you do it apart from Him. Hallelujah! I don't have to try anymore to do it myself because I know in advance it will be a failure if I do.

Then did you notice what follows right after that? "But if you stay in me and OBEY my commands, you may ask any request you like, and it will be granted!"

Do I need to say more? Who could help but want to OBEY Jesus when He gives you such a word as this, telling that you may ask any request you like, and it will be granted.

Thank You, Jesus!

John 16:24

"Ask, using my name, and you will receive, and your cup of joy will overflow."

Back up a little bit and read the verse before that where He says "At that time you won't need to ask me for anything, for you can go directly to the Father and ask him, and he will give you what you ask for because you use my name."

First you have a promise that you can ask and receive, but sometimes even greater than that is the very fact that in asking, not only will you receive, but your cup of JOY will overflow. Christians, the promise is there. All we have to do is accept it, because Jesus promises joy! Just imagine, joy comes from asking and receiving!

Another added bonus.

PETER

I Peter 5:7

"Let him have all your worries and cares, for he is always thinking about you and watching everything that concerns you."

Isn't it beautiful to know that we have someone who cares so much for us that he's willing to take all our worries and cares? Listen to this personalized and then spend a little time really thinking about the magnitude of this verse.

"Let him have all Frances' worries and cares, for he is always thinking about Frances and watching everything that concerns Frances."

He wants ALL my worries and cares—not just part of them, but ALL of them, and since He wants them, they don't belong to me any longer. To know that He is always thinking about me is almost incomprehensible to my mind. The God of all things, the great "I am" is always thinking about me (in spite of His busy schedule) and He is watching every single thing that concerns me. He cares about not only my spirit, but my body and my soul! He's not only watching me and protecting me, but He's watching every single thing that concerns me.

Thank You, Jesus. We sure don't deserve any of this, but it makes me love You even more to know that You care about EVERYTHING which concerns me. I will love You forever!

I Peter 1:14-15

>"Obey God because you are his children; don't slip back into your old ways—doing evil because you knew no better. But be holy now in everything you do, just as the Lord is holy, who invited you to be his child."

Don't we have a thrilling reason to obey God? This verse makes me bubble over with excitement, love, joy and peace because I don't have to obey God because He's sitting up there in heaven looking down at me, trying to catch me doing something wrong! No, it's my privilege to obey Him because I'm His child! Hallelujah! I AM HIS CHILD! I AM HIS CHILD!

There's so much in the Bible to encourage us to continue seeking more and more of God and not to return to our old ways, and what a promise of God! I AM HIS CHILD!

Making that fifteenth verse personal should give each and every one of us a desire to be more and more holy and more like God, because he personally invited us to be His child. Put your name in that last phrase, "just as the Lord is holy, who invited Frances Hunter to be his child." How could I ever want to disappoint Him when He personally invited me to be His child!

Thank You, Father, for looking to and fro and seeing me, and in spite of seeing what I was, personally inviting me to be Your child. I love You, love You, love You!

I Peter 1:18-19

>"God paid a ransom to save you from the impossible road to heaven which your fathers tried

to take, and the ransom he paid was not
mere gold or silver, as you very well know.
But he paid for you with the precious lifeblood of Christ, the sinless, spotless Lamb of
God."

Thank You, Lord. It's just like I'd been kidnapped and
put on the wrong road . . . the road leading right straight to
hell, but God Himself personally paid the ransom just to put
me on the impossible road to heaven. Hallelujah! And to
think He had all the gold and silver in the whole wide world,
and He could have used this as a ransom, but He didn't,
because He knew that wouldn't work, so He paid for me with
the only thing that was sufficient to pay the price—the
precious lifeblood of Christ, the sinless, spotless Lamb of
God.

If you want to get some spiritual goose pimples, put
your name in the nineteenth verse. "But he paid for Frances
Hunter with the precious lifeblood of Christ, the sinless
spotless Lamb of God."

How could we ever want to do anything but serve Him
in love and appreciation?

I Peter 1:23-25

"For you have a new life. It was not passed
on to you from your parents, for the life they gave
you will fade away. This new one will last forever,
for it comes from Christ, God's ever-living Message
to men.

"Yes, our natural lives will fade as grass does
when it becomes all brown and dry. All our
greatness is like a flower that droops and falls; but
the Word of the Lord will last forever. And his
message is the Good News that was preached to
you."

Some people have parents they feel they can be "proud" of. Others have parents they might have been ashamed of. Others don't even know who their parents are, but how beautiful is the fatherhood of those who have been born again because this verse tells us we have a NEW life. Not passed on to us by our parents, because that life is only temporary and will fade away. But, praise God, the new one will last forever because it comes from Jesus.

Praise God that even though our natural lives will fade as grass does, the Word of the Lord will last forever, and so will those of us who have believed and accepted His Word. There is no end, because eternity has no ending—We shall live forever!

I Peter 2:9-11

"... You have been chosen by God himself—you are priests of the King, you are holy and pure, you are God's very own—all this so that you may show to others how God called you out of the darkness into his wonderful light. Once you were less than nothing; now you are God's own. Once you knew very little of God's kindness; now your very lives have been changed by it.

"Dear brothers, you are only visitors here. Since your real home is in heaven I beg you to keep away from the evil pleasures of this world; they are not for you, for they fight against your very souls."

Can you imagine anything more wonderful than to know that you have been chosen by the Almighty God Himself and that He has made us priests, holy and pure. It is God who does the refining, but it is we who must be willing to let God make us holy and pure. Have you ever wished to return to the darkness now that you're in the light? Never, never, NEVER!

Isn't it glorious to know that our real home is not here where things can rust away, but this is only a temporary parking spot until we reach the Glory of God in heaven! Hallelujah!

Watch what happens when you make this verse personal: "Frances, you have been chosen by God himself— Frances, you are a priest of the King, you are holy and pure, Frances, you are God's very own—all this so that Frances can show to others how God called her out of the darkness into his wonderful light. Once Frnaces was less than nothing; now Frances is God's own. Once Frances knew very little of God's kindness; now her very life has been changed by it.

"Dear Frances, you are only a visitor here. Since your real home is in heaven I beg you to keep away from the evil pleasures of this world; they are not for Frances, for they fight against her very soul."

Substitute your name where I have put mine and let God speak to you and wee what it does to you.

I Peter 2:16

"You are free from the law, but that doesn't mean you are free to do wrong. Live as those who are free to do only God's will at all times."

How beautiful to know that you have complete freedom in the Lord—freedom to do everything He wants you to! Free from the law, but having the same freedom that keeps you from WANTING to do wrong. Praise God we are free to do only God's will at all times. We don't have to bow down to our old sinful natures and do what Satan wants us to do. We have complete freedom from those old obligations!

Praise You, Lord, for the liberty and freedom You give Your children.

I Peter 2:2-3

"Now that you realize how kind the Lord has been to you, put away all evil, deception, envy, and fraud. Long to grow up into the fullness of your salvation; cry for this as a baby cries for his milk."

This verse really speaks to me because of that last little phrase: "Cry for this as a baby cries for his milk." We all know the sound of a hungry baby, and that's the hunger we should have for the Word of God and for His goodness and kindness and mercy. And the Lord says: "Frances, now that you realize how kind the Lord has been to you, put away all evil, deception, envy, and fraud." He makes the Christian walk so easy because He really tells you what to do and what not to do, and then gives you a desire to do what He wants you to. Glory!

I Peter 5:7

"Let him have all your worries and cares, for he is always thinking about you and watching everything that concerns you."

Did you ever stop to meditate on the idea that God is *always* thinking about you? Can you imagine all the people God has to think about, and yet He is always thinking about you and watching everything that even concerns you. He's so anxious to protect His children He never takes His eyes off of us for a single moment. Did you ever realize that you were that important to God?

If you really want to feel the presence of God, make that verse personal: "Let him have all Frances' worries and cares, for he is always thinking about Frances and watching everything that concerns her."

What does that do to you?

II Peter 1:2-9

"Do you want more and more of God's kindness and peace? Then learn to know him better and better. For as you know him better, he will give you, through his great power, everything you need for living a truly good life: he even shares his own glory and his own goodness with us! And by that same mighty power he has given us all the other rich and wonderful blessings he promised; for instance, the promise to save us from the lust and rottenness all around us and to give us his own character.

"But to obtain these gifts, you need more than faith; you must also work hard to be good, and even that is not enough. For then you must learn to know God better and discover what he wants you to do.

"Next, learn to put aside your own desires so that you will become patient and godly, gladly letting God have his way with you. This will make possible the next step, which is for you to enjoy other people and to like them, and finally you will grow to love them deeply. The more you go on in this way, the more you will grow strong spiritually and become fruitful and useful to our Lord Jesus Christ. But anyone who fails to go after these additions to faith is blind indeed, or at least very shortsighted, and has forgotten that God delivered him from the old life of sin so that now he can live a strong, good life for the Lord."

God's instructions are so easy! It's so simple, it's so simple to live a Christian life, if we will only let Him speak to us through His Word. Look at that first verse! The question and then the simple answer of just getting to know Him better and better. And how can you get to know Him better and better? By spending more time with Him!

And then look what He promises—after you get to know Him better, He says He will give you everything you need for living a truly good life. God never intended that we had to do it on our own—He always intended to give us all the power and blessings we need!

Look at verse 5 at the last sentence. "For then you must learn to know God better and discover *what he wants you to do.*" Many people spend time asking God to bless some endeavor they thought of themselves, instead of asking God what He wants them to do. Seek God and find out what He wants out of your life, then look at verse 6. This is one of the hardest things for many people to learn to do—to just simply put aside your own desires so that you will become patient and godly, gladly letting God have His way with you. Putting down our own desires and dying to self is probably the most difficult step for most Christians, and yet it's so simple, because God makes immediate provisions for you when you do, but never before!

Let's all learn to do what God wants us to do! Let's make verse 5 personal. "Frances, you must learn to know God better and discover what he wants Frances to do." Simple little instruction, isn't it?

Let's try verse 6: "Next, Frances, you learn to put aside your own desires so that Frances will become patient and godly, gladly letting God have his way with her. This will make possible the next step, which is for Frances to enjoy other people and to like them, and finally she will grow to love them deeply. The more Frances goes on in this way, the more she will grow strong spiritually and become fruitful and useful to our Lord Jesus Christ. But if Frances fails to go after these additions to faith she is blind indeed, or at least very shortsighted, and has forgotten that God delivered Frances from the old life of sin so that now she can live a strong, good life for the Lord."

That's my part—putting aside my own desires and letting God have His way, and doesn't He spell it out so easy for us to understand?

Praise God! the instruction book is easy and glorious to read! Hallelujah!

THE REVELATION

There's a lot about this book that I don't really understand and yet this is one of my favorite "quick pick-ups" to read in the Bible. Somehow the awesome power and glory of God is reflected in this book as much as in any other book in the Bible. I have selected the verses here that are my very favorites, and I hope you will mark them with a marking pencil in your Bible and pick them up and read them when you need a real shot in the arm concerning the glory and majesty of God! I'm making no comments on these, but just asking you to look at what God promises you in this beautiful book of Revelation.

"To everyone who is victorious, I will give fruit from the Tree of Life in the Paradise of God." *(2:7)*

"Let everyone who can hear, listen to what the Spirit is saying to the churches: He who is victorious shall not be hurt by the Second Death." *(2:11)*

"Every one who is victorious shall eat of the hidden manna, the secret nourishment from heaven; and I will give to each a white stone, and on the stone will be engraved a

new name that no one else knows except the one receiving
it."   *(2:17)*

"To every one who overcomes—who to the very end
keeps on doing things that please me—I will give power over
the nations. You will rule them with a rod of iron just as my
Father gave me the authority to rule them; they will be
shattered like a pot of clay that is broken into tiny pieces.
And I will give you the Morning Star!"   *(2:26-28)*

"Everyone who conquers will be clothed in white, and I
will not erase his name from the Book of Life, but I will
announce before my Father and his angels that he is mine."
                                                                 (3:5)

"I know you well; you aren't strong, but you have tried
to obey and have not denied my Name. Therefore I have
opened a door to you that no one can shut."   *(3:8)*

"As for the one who conquers, I will make him a pillar
in the temple of my God; he will be secure, and will go out
no more; and I will write my God's Name on him, and he will
be a citizen in the city of my God—the New Jerusalem,
coming down from heaven from my God; and he will have
my new Name inscribed upon him."   *(3:12)*

"I know you well—you are neither hot nor cold; I wish
you were one or the other! But since you are merely
lukewarm, I will spit you out of my mouth!"   *(3:15)*

"Look! I have been standing at the door and I am
constantly knocking. If anyone hears me calling him and
opens the door, I will come in and fellowship with him and
he with me."   *(3:20)*

"I will let every one who conquers sit beside me on my throne, just as I took my place with my Father on his throne when I had conquered." *(3:21)*

"And instantly I was, in spirit, there in heaven and saw—oh, the glory of it! ... Great bursts of light flashed forth from him as from a glittering diamond, or from a shining ruby, and a rainbow glowing like an emerald encircled his throne." *(4:2-3)*

"Day after day and night after night they kept on saying, 'Holy, holy, holy, Lord God Almighty—the one who was, and is, and is to come.' And when the Living Beings gave glory and honor and thanks to the one sitting on the throne, who lives forever and ever, the twenty-four Elders fell down before him and worshiped him, the Eternal Living One, and cast their crowns before the throne, singing, 'O Lord, you are worthy to receive the glory and the honor and the power, for you have created all things. They were created and called into being by your act of will.' " *(4:8-11)*

" 'Who is worthy to break the seals on this scroll and to unroll it?' But no one in all heaven or earth or from among the dead was permitted to open and read it.

"Then I wept with disappointment because no one anywhere was worthy; no one could tell us what it said. But one of the twenty-four Elders said to me, 'Stop crying, for look! The Lion of the tribe of Judah, the Root of David, has conquered, and proved himself worthy to open the scroll and to break its seven seals.'

"I looked and saw a Lamb standing there before the twenty-four Elders, in front of the throne and the Living Beings, and on the Lamb were wounds that once had caused his death." *(5:2-6)*

"They were singing him a new song with these words: 'You are worthy to take the scroll and break its seals and open it; for you were slain, and your blood has bought people from every nation as gifts for God. And you have gathered them into a kingdom and made them priests of our God; they shall reign upon the earth.'

"Then in my vision I heard the singing of millions of angels surrounding the throne and the Living Beings and the Elders: 'The Lamb is worthy' (loudly they sang it!) '—the Lamb who was slain. He is worthy to receive the power, and the riches, and the wisdom, and the strength, and the honor, and the glory, and the blessing.'

"And then I heard everyone in heaven and earth, and from the dead beneath the earth and in the sea, exclaiming, 'The blessing and the honor and the glory and the power belong to the one sitting on the throne, and to the Lamb forever and ever.' And the four Living Beings kept saying, 'Amen!' And the twenty-four Elders fell down and worshiped him."

(5:9-14)

"The kings of the earth, and world leaders and rich men, and high-ranking military officers, and all men great and small, slave and free, hid themselves in the caves and rocks of the mountains, and cried to the mountains to crush them. 'Fall on us,' they pleaded, 'and hide us from the face of the one sitting on the throne, and from the anger of the Lamb, because the great day of their anger has come, and who can survive it?' "

(6:15-17)

"Then locusts came from the smoke and descended onto the earth and were given power to sting like scorpions. They were told not to hurt the grass or plants or trees, but to attack those people who did not have the mark of God on their foreheads. They were not to kill them, but to torture them for five months with agony like the pain of scorpion stings. In those days men will try to kill themselves but won't

be able to—death will not come. They will long to die—but
death will flee away!"   *(9:3-6)*

"But the men left alive after these plagues still refused
to worship God! They would not renounce their demon-
worship, nor their idols made of gold and silver, brass, stone
and wood—which neither see nor hear nor walk! Neither did
they change their mind and attitude about all their murders
and witchcraft, their immorality and theft."   *(9:20-21)*

"But after three and a half days, the spirit of life from
God will enter them and they will stand up! And great fear
will fall on everyone."   *(11:11)*

"Then I heard again what sounded like the shouting of a
huge crowd, or like the waves of a hundred oceans crashing
on the shore, or like the mighty rolling of great thunder.
'Praise the Lord. For the Lord our God, the Almighty, reigns.
Let us be glad and rejoice and honor him; for the time has
come for the wedding banquet of the Lamb, and his bride has
prepared herself.'"   *(19:16)*

In his mouth he held a sharp sword to strike down the
nations; he ruled them with an iron grip; and he trod the
winepress of the fierceness of the wrath of Almighty God. On
his robe and thigh was written this title: 'King of Kings and
Lord of Lords.'"   *(19:15)*

"He will wipe away all tears from their eyes, and there
shall be no more death, nor sorrow, nor crying, nor pain. All
of that has gone forever."   *(21:4)*

"In a vision he took me to a towering mountain peak
and from there I watched that wondrous city, the holy
Jerusalem, descending out of the skies from God. It was filled
with the glory of God, and flashed and glowed like a precious

gem, crystal clear like jasper. Its walls were broad and high, with twelve gates guarded by twelve angels." *(21:10-12)*

"No temple could be seen in the city, for the Lord God Almighty and the Lamb are worshiped in it everywhere. And the city has no need of sun or moon to light it, for the glory of God and of the Lamb illuminate it. Its light will light the nations of the earth, and the rulers of the world will come and bring their glory to it. Its gates never close; they stay open all day long—and there is no night! And the glory and honor of all the nations shall be brought into it. Nothing evil will be permitted in it—no one immoral or dishonest—but only those whose names are written in the Lamb's Book of Life." *(21:22-27)*

"And he pointed out to me a river of pure Water of Life, clear as crystal, flowing from the throne of God and the Lamb, coursing down the center of the main street. On each side of the river grew Trees of Life, bearing twelve crops of fruit, with a fresh crop each month; the leaves were used for medicine to heal the nations.

"There shall be nothing in the city which is evil; for the throne of God and of the Lamb will be there, and his servants will worship him. And they shall see his face; and his name shall be written on their foreheads. And there will be no night there—no need for lamps or sun—for the Lord God will be their light; and they shall reign forever and ever." *(22:1-5)*

"Then he instructed me, 'Do not seal up what you have written, for the time of fulfillment is near. And when that time comes, all doing wrong will do it more and more; the vile will become more vile; good men will be better; those who are holy will continue on in greater holiness.'"

(22:10-11)

"The Spirit and the bride say, 'Come.' Let each one who hears them say the same, 'Come.' Let the thirsty one come—anyone who wants to; let him come and drink the Water of Life without charge."   *(22:17)*

I hope these verses have done as much for you as they do for me, because when I finish reading these verses in Revelation, I always feel like John did in the first chapter, verse 17: "When I saw him, *I fell at his feet as dead.*" What a promise to know that some day we'll see our glorious Savior face to face; and isn't it hard to imagine what we'll feel like or what we'll say on that glorious occasion. I think John did the thing that most of us will do . . . we will fall at his feet as dead! Hallelujah! Maranatha!

Revelation 1:10, 17

"I was in the Spirit on the Lord's day. . . .
And when I saw him, I fell at his feet as dead."
(From the *King James* version)

If you really want to be "in the Spirit," there's nothing like Bible reading to put you right there. There is where you find a complete disassociation with the "world" and a knowledge that goes beyond plain knowledge that it's just "you and me, Lord!" The times in our lives when Charles and I have been the closest to God have been the times when we have been so "in the Spirit" we weren't even aware of anything in the entire world, a state from which we hate to return. Somehow I find in reading God's Word, and getting completely absorbed in it for an hour or more, can be some of the greatest worship time of my life—because as I read God's promises to me I have no other choice than to worship Him to the fullest extent of my being. This is that sacred time when God reveals so much of His plan for my life (and He will for you, too), and when our relationship is at its very peak.

I think of John and how the book of Revelation was given to him and how it all started in his complete absorption and worship of God. Would you like to read, trying to understand as best you can, how completely he was "in the Spirit" when he "fell at his feet as dead"? He says, "It was the Lord's Day and I was worshiping" (*The Living Bible* translation). Can you imagine the extent of his worship at that time? It wasn't a nominal Christian's worship on Sunday morning, it was a complete absorption in the things of God, with everything else excluded from his mind.

If you will read this part out loud I think you'll receive one of the greatest blessings of your life. May we all search to be as completely in the Spirit so that we too can fall at His feet as dead in complete worship and adoration.

Revelation 1:9-17

I was on the island of Patmos, exiled there for preaching the Word of God, and for telling what I knew about Jesus Christ. It was the Lord's Day and I was worshiping, when suddenly I heard a loud voice behind me, a voice that sounded like a trumpet blast, saying, 'I am A and Z, the First and Last!' And then I heard him say, 'Write down everything you see, and send your letter to the seven churches in Turkey: to the church in Ephesus, the one in Smyrna, and those in Pergamos, Thyatira, Sardis, Philadelphia, and Laodicea.'

When I turned to see who was speaking, there behind me were seven candlesticks of gold. And standing among them was one who looked like Jesus who called himself the Son of Man, wearing a long robe circled with a golden band across his chest. His hair was white as wool or snow, and his eyes penetrated like flames of fire. His feet gleamed like burnished bronze, and his voice thundered like the waves against the shore. He held seven stars in his right hand and a sharp, double-bladed sword in his mouth, and his face shone like the power of the sun in unclouded brilliance.

"When I saw him, I fell at his feet as dead."

MATTHEW
(HOW DO YOU TREAT
MY SON JESUS)

One of my exciting Christian experiences "happened" in a most unusual way. Charles and I had been to a powerful meeting and had seen the power of God work through an evangelist in a greater way than we had ever witnessed in our entire lives. We asked him the secret of the power and he simply said: "I spend at least eight hours every day in God's Word. There is no power without that!" That stunned me—I thought of my own life with letters to answer, clothes to wash, food to be bought at the stores, a house to clean, and wondered how I could ever find time to spend eight hours in one uninterrupted stretch in God's Holy Word. This had put such a hungering in my heart, that I prayed and said, "God, would You please give me at least *one* day in my hurried life to spend an uninterrupted eight-hour day with just You and me?"

We ought to always be careful how we pray, because God recognizes a sincere heart, and will do all kinds of things to see that our prayer is answered, as I found out a little later, in this adventure I share with you.

I was scheduled to be in a little town in Kansas. In order to get there I had to leave Houston early in the morning, stop in Dallas, wait for another plane, and then just hedge-hop all the way until I got to Liberal, Kansas, where I was to be met and driven to the small town. Although the distance was not long, the flight was, because of the several connections. I boarded the plane in Houston well armed for the long flight with my *Living Bible.* I started in Matthew and had a very unusual experience, because as I finished the book for the first time, God spoke softly and said, "Go back and read it again." So I did. Then God said to read it again, and finally the fourth time.

In the meantime, I was seated in the small plane taking me to the final stop in Kansas. But somehow in that special way we have of knowing when God's going to do something special in our lives, I knew that something unusual was happening now, and I continued reading and rereading the book of Matthew. Then I heard the small, still voice of God say, "Let Me speak to you while you read it again." I began to read again and to listen intently.

All of a sudden God said, "Wherever you go, ask them how do they treat My Son Jesus?"

DO YOU YIELD TO TEMPTATION?
Matthew 4:1-10

I continued reading, because I knew there was more to come. Nothing happened in the first three chapters, and then after I read the first ten verses in Chapter 4:

> "Then Jesus was led out into the wilderness by the Holy Spirit, to be tempted there by Satan. For forty days and forty nights he ate nothing and became very hungry. Then Satan tempted him to get food by changing stones into loaves of bread.
> .'' 'It will prove you are the Son of God,' he said.
> "But Jesus told him, 'No! For the Scriptures tell us that bread won't feed men's souls: obedience to every word of God is what we need.'

"Then Satan took him to Jerusalem to the roof of the Temple. 'Jump off,' he said, 'and prove you are the Son of God; for the Scriptures declare, 'God will send his angels to keep you from harm,' . . . they will prevent you from smashing on the rocks below.'

"Jesus retorted, 'It also says not to put the Lord your God to a foolish test!'

"Next Satan took him to the peak of a very high mountain and showed him the nations of the world and all their glory.

" 'I'll give it all to you,' he said, 'If you will only kneel and worship me.'

" 'Get out of here, Satan,' Jesus told him. 'The Scriptures say, 'Worship only the Lord God. Obey only him.' ' "

I heard God say: "Ask them, 'Do you yield to temptation? . . . Do YOU yield to temptation?' "

INSTANT OBEDIENCE
Matthew 4:19-22

I read on, because I knew there was more to come. I didn't have to wait long! I read:

"Jesus called out, 'Come along with me and I will show you how to fish for the souls of men!' And they left their nets at once and went with him.

"A little farther up the beach he saw two other brothers, James and John, sitting in a boat with their father Zebedee, mending their nets; and he called to them to come too. At once they stopped their work and, leaving their father behind, went with him."

And again God spoke and I heard Him say: "Ask them, do they INSTANTLY obey? . . . Ask them, do they instantly OBEY?"

Matthew 5:21-22

I read on, anxious to find out what the next thing God was going to talk about. When I got to this part, I knew something exciting was going to happen:

"Under the laws of Moses the rule was, 'If you kill, you must die.' But I have added to that rule, and tell you that if you are only *angry*, even in your own home, you are in danger of judgment! If you call your friend an idiot, you are in danger of being brought before the court. And if you curse him, you are in danger of the fires of hell."

And then I heard God speak again. "Ask them," He said, "Do you have ought against your brother?"
Do you have ought against your brother?

Matthew 6:25-33

I read on, and the suspense continued to grow as I anxiously kept reading to find out what God had in full to say on this chapter:

"So my counsel is: Don't worry about *things*—food, drink, and clothes. For you already have life and a body—and they are far more important than what to eat and wear. Look at the birds! They don't worry about what to eat—they don't need to sow or reap or store up food—for your heavenly Father feeds them. And you are far more valuable to him than they are. Will all your worries add a single moment to your life?

"And why worry about your clothes? Look at the field lilies! They don't worry about theirs. Yet King Solomon in all his glroy was not clothed as beautifully as they. And if God cares so wonderfully for flowers that are here today and gone tomorrow, won't he more surely care for you, O men of little faith?

"So don't worry at all about having enough food and clothing. Why be like the heathen? For they take pride in all these things and are deeply concerned about them. But your heavenly Father already knows perfectly well that you need them, and he will give them to you if you give him first place in your life and live as he wants you to."

And then God spoke and said, "Ask them, 'Do you worry? Do you trust Me? Do you really believe?' "

Do you worry? (That's for the heathens.) Do you trust Him? Do you really believe?

My heart cried out—"Oh, God, there are so many Christians who worry and worry about everything. What can I say to them?"

And He simply answered: "Ask them if they trust Me!"

Matthew 7:21

The plane was getting close to landing time by now, and I hurriedly read on, anxious to see what God was going to say next! I read on.

"Not all who sound religious are really godly people. They may refer to me as 'Lord,' but still won't get to heaven. For the decisive question is whether they obey my Father in heaven."

God's voice softly whispered, "Ask them, 'Do they really obey?' Do they REALLY obey? Do they really OBEY?"

By this time, I heard something over the loudspeaker that shocked me. It never happened to me before, nor has it ever happened since. At the sound of the pilot's voice, I looked out the window and it looked like we were smothered in red dust. . . . I didn't know what it was, and then I heard the pilot say: "Because of the dust storm, we are unable to land at Liberal, and will continue on to Denver."

I rang for the hostess and said, "I've got to get off at Liberal—there are people waiting down there for me to speak at a city-wide meeting tonight. How can I get back from Denver? I've never missed a speaking date in my life!" She simply smiled and said she was sorry there was nothing they could do about it, but continue on to Denver.

I went back to reading the Bible, secretly delighted because I would have more time to spend with Jesus.

Matthew 8:1-4

I read on.

"Large crowds followed Jesus as he came down the hillside.

"Look! A leper is approaching. He kneels before him, worshiping. 'Sir,' the leper pleads, 'if you want to, you can heal me.'

"Jesus touches the man. 'I want to,' he says, 'be healed.' And instantly the leprosy disappears.

"Then Jesus says to him, 'Don't stop to talk to anyone; go right over to the priest to be examined; and take with you the offering required by Moses' law for lepers who are healed—a public testimony of your cure.' "

When I got to this part, I heard that same voice again saying: "Ask them . . . ask them . . . 'Do you ALWAYS testify? Do you always TESTIFY?' " Shivers ran up and down my back when I realized how many times we fail to testify about the great things God has done for us.

Matthew 9:9

I read on.

> "As Jesus was going on down the road, he saw a tax collector, Matthew, sitting at a tax collection booth. 'Come and be my disciple,' Jesus said to him, and Matthew jumped up and went along with him."

At the end of that little verse, God spoke again and said: "Ask them again . . . 'Do YOU instantly obey?' " Again He repeated the question. "Ask them again, 'Do you IN-STANTLY obey?' "

Matthew 9:37-38

By this time I was only aware of two people—God and me! No one else on the plane—the stewardess or anyone else. I could have been in the middle of a desert for all I knew. I read on.

> "The harvest is so great, and the workers are so few," he told his disciples. "So pray to the one in charge of the harvesting, and ask him to recruit more workers for his harvest fields."

God whispered: "Ask them, 'Are they willing to be recruited?' . . . Ask them, 'Are they WILLING to be recruited?' "

Are you?

Matthew 10:37

I read on, oblivious to time or place.

"If you love your father and mother more
than you love me, you are not worthy of being
mine; or if you love your son or daughter more
than me, you are not worthy of being mine."

There was a tremendous love of God enveloping me as I
read this particular part, and I knew something real special
was coming next.

God said: "Ask them, 'Who do you love the most? Who
comes FIRST in your life?' "

Who do you put first in your life?

Matthew 12:34

I read on, devouring every single word, to be sure I
wouldn't miss what God had to say next.

"You brood of snakes! How could evil men
like you speak what is good and right? For a man's
heart determines his speech."

Softly He whispered, "Ask them, 'What comes out of
YOUR mouth?' "

I thought about my own mouth. I thought about
what I had heard from the lips of other Christians, and
wondered if all that came out of our mouths was of
God?

Matthew 13:45-46

I read on. Soon there was a stirring in my heart as I got
here.

"Again, the Kingdom of Heaven is like a pearl merchant on the lookout for choice pearls. He discovered a real bargain—a pearl of great value—and sold everything he owned to purchase it!"

Then He said: "Ask them, 'Are they willing to give ALL?' "
"Ask them, 'Are they really willing to give all?' "

Matthew 14:25-33

Every question I heard Him say to ask made me search my own heart too! I excitedly read on.

"About four o'clock in the morning Jesus came to them, walking on the water! They screamed in terror, for they thought he was a ghost.
"But Jesus immediately spoke to them, re-assuring them. 'Don't be afraid!' he said.
"Then Peter called to him: 'Sir, if it is really you, tell me to come over to you, walking on the water.'
" 'All right,' the Lord said, 'come along!'
"So Peter went over the side of the boat and walked on the water toward Jesus. But when he looked around at the high waves, he was terrified and began to sink. 'Save me, Lord!' he shouted.
"Instantly Jesus reached out his hand and rescued him. 'O man of little faith,' Jesus said. 'Why did you doubt me?' And when they had climbed back into the boat, the wind stopped.
"The others sat there, awestruck. 'You really are the Son of God!' they exclaimed."

Then He said: "Ask them, 'Do they really trust Me?' "
"Ask them, 'Do they really TRUST Me?' "

Matthew 16:24-26

I read on quickly now because it seemed there would be a little pause between His voice. Then I read:

> "Then Jesus said to the disciples, 'If anyone wants to be a follower of mine, let him deny himself and take up his cross and follow me. For anyone who keeps his life for himself shall lose it; and anyone who loses his life for me shall find it again. What profit is there if you gain the whole world—and lose eternal life? What can be compared with the value of eternal life?' "

And He said: "Ask them again and again, the most important question of all, 'Are they really willing to give all?' *Every single thing to belong to Me?*"

Matthew 18:1-3

I read on, my interest growing more and more all the time.

> "About that time the disciples came to Jesus to ask which of them would be greatest in the Kingdom of Heaven!
> "Jesus called a small child over to him and set the little fellow down among them, and said, 'Unless you turn to God from your sins and become as little children, you will never get into the Kingdom of Heaven.' "

God said, "Ask them, 'Are you willing to come as a little child? In simple faith? Are you?' "

Matthew 19:4-6

I read on.

" 'Don't you read the Scriptures?' he replied. 'In them it is written that at the beginning God created man and woman, and that a man should leave his father and mother, and be forever united to his wife. The two shall become one—no longer two, but one! And no man may divorce what God has joined together.' "

Then God said: "Ask them, 'Do they really believe in marriage?' " I thought about all the married couples I had counseled with and all the problems they were having, and I thought of how easily they were thinking of divorce, and my heart cried at the answer a lot of people would have to give to that question.

Matthew 22:37

I read on.

"Jesus replied, 'Love the Lord your God with all your heart, soul, and mind. This is the first and greatest commandment. The second most important is similar: Love your neighbor as much as you love yourself.' "

Then God said: "Ask them again and again, 'Who do you love the most? Who do you put first in your life?' "

Matthew 24:30-41

I read on. Soon I knew it was time for more!

"And then at last the signal of my coming will appear in the heavens and there will be deep mourning all around the earth. And the nations of the world will see me arrive in the clouds of heaven, with power and great glory. And I shall send forth my angels with the sound of a mighty trumpet blast, and they shall gather my chosen ones from the farthest ends of the earth and heaven.

"Now learn a lesson from the fig tree. When her branch is tender and the leaves begin to sprout, you know that summer is almost here. Just so, when you see all these things beginning to happen, you can know that my return is near, even at the doors. Then at last this age will come to its close.

"Heaven and earth will disappear, but my words remain forever. But no one knows the date and hour when the end will be—not even the angels. No, nor even God's Son. Only the Father knows.

"The world will be at ease—banquets and parties and weddings—just as it was in Noah's time before the sudden coming of the flood; people wouldn't believe what was going to happen until the flood actually arrived and took them all away. So shall my coming be.

"Two men will be working together in the fields, and one will be taken, the other left. Two women will be going about their household tasks; one will be taken, the other left."

God said: "What will you be doing? . . . Ask them, 'What will you be doing?' "

Matthew 26:7

I continued on.

> "While he was eating, a woman came in with a bottle of very expensive perfume, and poured it over his head."

God said: "She gave the best she had. Would you? . . . Ask them, 'Would you give the best you had?'"

Matthew 27:26-30

I heard nothing again until I got almost through the twenty-seventh chapter:

> "Then Pilate released Barabbas to them. And after he had whipped Jesus, he gave him to the Roman soldiers to take away and crucify. But first they took him into the armory and called out the entire contingent. They stripped him and put a scarlet robe on him, and made a crown from long thorns and put it on his head, and placed a stick in his right hand as a scepter and knelt before him in mockery. 'Hail, King of the Jews,' they yelled. And they spat on him and grabbed the stick and beat him on the head with it."

I cried as I read this because I could almost feel the beating on my own back as I read what they did to Jesus. This was the divine Son of God. How could they do that to Him? My heart sobbed and sobbed as I thought about Jesus. I could feel the crown made of long thorns being literally pushed into His head. And when I read that they "spat" on Him and grabbed the stick and beat Him on the head with it, my own soul was in agony. They spat upon Jesus! I had never felt this particular passage this vividly before, and now I know why.

God spoke saying, "Ask them, 'How do they treat My Son Jesus?'" I looked around the airplane and saw the cigarette smoke filtering up to the top of the plane. I heard the cocktail glasses tinkling with the ice in them. I thought about the indifference to God viewed everywhere and wondered which was worse. Spitting on Him, or just ignoring Him.

God spoke again and said, "Ask them in every city you go, 'How do THEY treat My Son Jesus?'"

I read to the end of the book. There was no more. I turned back to the first page of the book of Matthew and wrote the date and the following: "Ask them, 'How do THEY treat My Son Jesus?'"

Before our conversation ended, I had landed in Denver, checked to see about the possibilities of returning to Liberal, discovered that nothing was landing there. The airlines gave me a "futile trip fare" and sent me back to Houston. Somewhere between Denver and Houston God finished talking to me about Matthew.

When I landed at Houston, I looked at my watch—it was exactly ten hours from the time I left Houston in the morning. God had answered my prayer for eight uninterrupted hours with Him in a most unique way! High up in the sky, on April 12, 1972 . . . a day I will never forget! The airlines returned my total fare since it was a "futile trip." They thought I hadn't gone anywhere!

I knew differently—I had lain in the bosom of God for ten beautiful hours!

I was in the Spirit . . . and heard!

How do *you* treat My Son JESUS?